Brit.sh Imperial and For

18

John Aldred

Series Editors
Martin Collier
Rosemary Rees

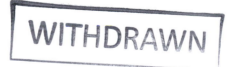
Heinemann

HEINEMANN ADVANCED HISTORY

Heinemann Educational Publishers
Halley Court, Jordan Hill, Oxford OX2 8EJ
Part of Harcourt Education

Heinemann is the registered trademark of
Harcourt Education Limited

© John Aldred, 2004

First published 2004

09 08 07 06 05 04
10 9 8 7 6 5 4 3 2 1

British Library Cataloguing in Publication Data is available from the British Library on request.

ISBN 0 435 32753 4

Typeset by TechType, Abingdon, Oxon

Original illustrations © Harcourt Education Limited, 2004
Illustrated TechType, Abingdon, Oxon
Cover design by hicksdesign
Printed in UK by Bath Press Ltd.
Cover photo: © Punch
Picture research by Sally Cole

Acknowledgements
The author and the publisher would like to thank the following for permission to reproduce photographs: pp. 17, 23, 31, 38, 131 Punch; pp. 44, 60 Mary Evans Picture Library; p. 58 (top and bottom) Richard Opie; p. 61 National Library of Scotland; pp. 64, 88, 90 (top), 92, 104 Hulton Archive; pp. 90 (bottom), 93 Popperfoto; pp. 102, 118 Centre for study of cartoons & caricatures University of Kent; p. 159 Bodleian Library.

Tables: p. 7 Chris Cook and John Stevenson, *The Longman Handbook of Modern British History 1714-1980*, Longman (1983), p. 186; p. 116 Chris Cook and John Stevenson, *The Longman Handbook of Modern British History 1714-1980*, Longman (1983), p. 189; p. 144 Alan Farmer, *Britain: Foreign and Imperial Affairs 1919-39*, Hodder and Stoughton (1992), p. 52.

Every effort has been made to contact copyright holders of material reproduced in this book. Any omissions will be rectified in subsequent printings if notice is given to the publishers.

This book is dedicated, with love, to my wife, Nicola.

CONTENTS

HOW TO USE THIS BOOK

This book is divided into an AS section and an A2 section.

The AS section contains a detailed descriptive analysis focused on British imperial and foreign policy between 1846 and 1963. Each chapter title is framed as a key question, which is then answered in the text. In addition to this, there are further key questions raised in each chapter so that the reader's attention is continually drawn towards analytical thinking as well as purely descriptive detail. At the end of each chapter there are additional questions, which enable the reader to use the content to explain, evaluate and analyse important issues covered in the chapter.

The A2 section is more analytical. The focus is on British imperial policy and each section addresses a specific theme which spans the nineteenth and twentieth centuries. There are direct links between this section and the AS section. The A2 section is designed to develop greater analytical understanding, based on the groundwork set out in the AS section. An example of this is that a student who reads Chapters 1, 4 and 7 will develop some knowledge and understanding of economic factors in imperialism. This theme is then examined analytically in Section 2.

At the end of the AS and A2 sections there are Assessment Questions. These are directly linked to examination board specifications and they are in the style of questions set by the major examining boards. In addition to the questions, there is also a detailed summary of how the questions should be approached. The emphasis is upon examination technique to enable the students to make the best use of their knowledge and understanding.

The bibliography is focused on the key references that students could draw upon in order to extend their knowledge and understanding of the issues and themes covered in this book.

The rise and fall of Britain's imperial power

A young Victoria ascended the throne in 1837 and began a reign that was to last for 64 years. By the time her reign ended in 1901, the British Empire had vastly increased in size and geographic distribution. In addition to consolidating its hold over Canada, Australia and the Indian sub-continent, Britain had established imperial strongholds across Africa, South East Asia and the Pacific.

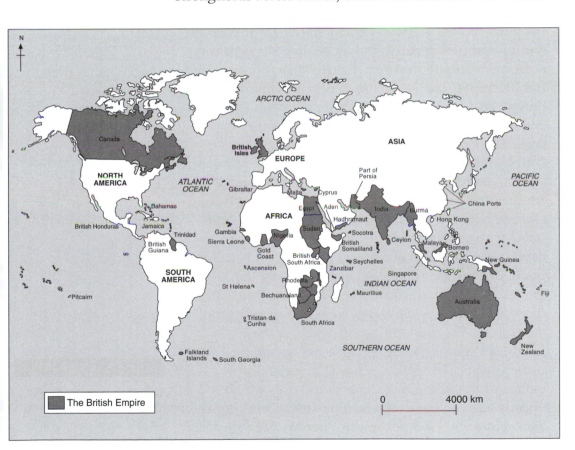

The extent of the British Empire in 1914

Before the First World War, the empire was of supreme importance for Britain. It gave the **mother country**:

- Global influence – In a pre-nuclear, Euro-centred power structure, Britain was able to project its influence anywhere in the world. The British Empire was defended by the world's mightiest navy and, in India alone, 340,000 troops. The scale of the empire was an ever-present measure of Britain's status as a great power.
- Economic prosperity – Between 1870 and 1914, the empire became a vital contributor to British industrial export growth. By 1914, over a third of British exports went to the empire. This dependency upon imperial trade became even more important for Britain's economic survival between World War I and II. British investors and big business became important influences on imperial policy, particularly regarding the expansion of Britain's empire in Africa. British financiers benefited from lucrative investments in mining precious metals, railway building and the extractive industries. The empire brought work to Britain and its people, particularly the British working class.
- National morale – The British people, for the most part, were united through a common sense of patriotism. The empire served to generate support for the British ruling class. In many respects, the empire brought enhanced stability to the British political system through a developed perception of national identity and national pride. Britons saw themselves as members of the greatest nation on earth and the British navy did 'rule the waves'. The middle classes were avid supporters of the empire. The working class less so, but they recognised their dependency upon the empire for employment. The working class were generally interested in issues closer to home and ones which directly affected them. For example, many working-class men volunteered to fight in **the Boer War** (1899–1902) as a means of escaping poverty rather than because they were deeply committed to protecting the empire.

Despite these benefits, even before 1914, the empire was showing signs of strain. Defence costs were a key issue. The geographic spread of the empire demanded an expensive naval defence system. New imperial rivals, such as

Germany, emerged to challenge Britain's power and increase the costs of defending the empire. By 1901, Britain was spending twice as much as Germany and France on imperial defence. The British Empire was not only larger than those of Germany and France, it was also geographically scattered which heightened the costs of protecting it. Protection of the empire was a primary objective of British foreign policy in the late nineteenth century. The perceived threats to imperial security came from the French in Africa and the Russians in the Far East.

The turning point for the British Empire came with the First World War. This left Britain as a debtor nation and it raised the question as to whether Britain could afford to maintain such a vast imperial commitment. In this framework of economic weakness, another problem beset Britain's empire. It was a patchwork of radically contrasting political, constitutional and economic structures at different points of development. To add to the problem there was no clearly defined plan as to how Britain's post-war relationship with its empire would develop. Furthermore, the **self-governing dominions** increasingly demanded independence from British rule.

By 1945, the British imperial system was finished. The Second World War marked the beginning of the end of empire, and the loss of India marked the first step in that decline. Empire was no longer relevant, it was too costly to maintain and it was impossible for Britain to ignore, or accommodate, the ever-rising tide of nationalism.

THE DECLINE OF BRITAIN AS A GREAT POWER

Power was focused in Europe until 1914. The measure of that power was colonial strength, economic wealth and military might. Since 1846, Britain's policies were geared towards ensuring that these criteria were in place and that any threats to weaken them, such as **Soviet aggression in Europe**, would be dealt with effectively. The danger of aggressive rivalry from Germany became a serious problem by the start of the twentieth century. By 1918 Britain's status as a great power and the assumption that world power was centred in Europe had been undermined. Britain had emerged from war facing huge debts and with an empire that was less stable than at any other time.

KEY TERM

Self-governing dominions
Some colonies were given a form of limited independence. Britain kept control over defence and foreign policy, but in all other matters the colonies had self-governing dominion status, meaning they were free from direct control from Britain. Between 1840 and 1872, Canada, Australia, Cape Colony and New Zealand achieved dominion status.

KEY THEME

Soviet aggression in Europe Britain was convinced that there was a Soviet intention to spread communism and Soviet influence throughout Europe after the Second World War.

Post-1918 foreign policy was a clear indicator of Britain's changed status. This was most graphically illustrated through appeasement. Even though, by 1918, it appeared as if Britain's rivals had been irreversibly weakened, the reality was very different. Germany's economic recovery after 1933 appeared to be remarkable. Britain's economy was stagnant and in no condition to back any serious challenge to German rearmament. To add to Britain's fundamental weakness, **the League of Nations** had also failed to restrain German ambitions in Europe before 1939. Its members were disunited and they lacked the political will and the economic means to keep Germany's **aggressive nationalism** in check.

In 1935, Britain agreed to allow Germany to increase its naval power to 35 per cent of the size of the British navy. This reinforced the limitations of British power and represented a fundamental breach of **the Treaty of Versailles**.

By 1945, power had shifted from Europe to a new **bi-polar balance**. The USA had emerged as the dominant superpower and Britain was faced with having its influence expressed through a close alliance with the USA, rather than acting as a key player in its own right. The criteria defining national and international power had dramatically changed.

SUMMARY QUESTIONS

1. Why did Britain's empire expand in the nineteenth century and contract in the twentieth century?

2. Explain two reasons why Britain had declined as a great power by 1945.

KEY ORGANISATION

The League of Nations
This was created through the Treaty of Versailles in 1919. Its main aim was to preserve peace through collective security and international cooperation.

KEY TERM

Aggressive nationalism
The use of force to achieve national strength. By attacking neighbouring states, Germany was able to reinforce its own power. Such attacks were justified in Nazi thinking because the strong have a natural right to prey upon the weak.

KEY TREATY

The Treaty of Versailles, 1919 The victorious powers, Britain and France, imposed this treaty on Germany after the First World War. Much of it was designed to prevent Germany starting another war, but its terms were regarded by many Germans as a harsh and excessive punishment.

KEY TERM

Bi-polar balance The two superpowers emerged in the form of the Soviet Union and the USA. These two power bases were diametrically opposed to each other, like the opposite poles of a compass.

CHAPTER 1

What principles guided Britain's foreign and imperial policies between 1846 and 1902?

The foundations of British foreign policy towards Europe had been laid in 1815. The European great powers, of whom Britain was one, had established the **Concert of Europe**. Commitment to this was to be of primary importance to Britain for at least the next 50 years.

The Concert was a purely European arrangement, but Britain's interests extended well beyond Europe. Nevertheless, throughout the nineteenth century there was a direct link between order in Europe and the protection and expansion of the British Empire. A strategically and diplomatically stable Europe not only enabled Britain to retain its status as a regional and continental power, but also as an imperial power. This relationship between European peace and British imperial power was a central factor that drove Britain's foreign and imperial policies throughout most of the nineteenth century. There was a degree of consistency in the principles on which the policies were based, but the methods employed to ensure that Britain's vital national interests were guaranteed changed over time.

WHAT WAS THE BALANCE OF POWER IN EUROPE?

From 1846 to 1902, one of Britain's primary objectives was to maintain a **balance of power** in Europe. Throughout this period, Britain was only involved in one European war, **the Crimean War** (1854–6), fought to enforce and maintain the balance of power in Europe. The preservation of this stability was dependent upon a willingness by Britain and the other Great Powers of Europe to:

- recognise the central importance for all of them of preserving peace, order and balance in Europe
- put this objective above the national interests of individual states
- agree that no state should increase its territorial size or its political influence in Europe unless the other great powers agreed to it

- prevent a weak and vulnerable state from becoming the victim of a stronger aggressor
- take joint action, including war if necessary, against any state whose actions might threaten to upset the balance
- respect treaties, which have been agreed to as part of the preservation of the balance of power.

Why was the European balance of power so important for Britain?

There was a direct link between British foreign policy in Europe and Britain's global imperial policy. Both strands of government action were founded upon economic priorities.

- Foreign wars were expensive and the outcomes were often unpredictable. Peace was financially cheap. Inevitably, the costs of wars were met through taxation and government borrowing. Diplomacy rather than military force was a far cheaper way of protecting Britain's vital national interests, particularly in an age when economic growth, rather than military spending, was a priority for the British ruling class and its **entrepreneurial** supporters.
- By 1850, Britain was a major exporting nation. Most of Britain's trade was with North America, Africa and the Pacific, which were also the main areas of investment. These lucrative markets needed to be protected by a large and expensive navy. A considerable amount of naval activity occurred along the coast of West Africa to prevent the slave trade. A peaceful and stable Europe contributed towards Britain's ability to fund its navy and thereby protect trade and the national economic prosperity to which it contributed.
- Britain's status as a great European power had been established and fixed in 1815. Any significant change in the distribution of power in Europe could threaten that status. Status as a European power complimented and supported Britain's status as an imperial power. Without stability in Europe and continuity in the distribution of power in Europe, Britain's ability to project itself as a regional and global power would have been under threat. One alternative strategy to adopt when the balance of power in Europe was less certain after 1865 was for Britain to embark on a massive expansion of its

KEY TERM

Entrepreneurial The practice of investing in new ideas and taking risks by supporting new economic ventures. The rewards for success were usually very high.

imperial power in order to counter the challenge from rivals in Europe.

- Britain's priority was to preserve its international status. This was not necessarily to be achieved by the preservation of the map of Europe fixed in 1815. The key principle underlying Britain's policy was that any changes in the territorial balance should not result in a relative decline in Britain's international status.

PROTECTING OVERSEAS TRADE AND THE ECONOMY

An examination of the British economy and Britain's position as a trading nation amply explains why these were so important as determining factors influencing foreign and imperial policy. Economic wealth and **global trade dominance** were essential criteria in determining great power status. It was a guiding principle of British imperial and foreign policy that they should remain a great power.

Mid-Victorian prosperity, 1851–73

This period was one of unprecedented growth in the development of the British economy. Between 1854 and 1860 economic growth averaged 1.7% and this rose to 3.6% between 1861 and 1865 and 2.1% between 1866 and 1874.

Britain's staple industries (coal, cotton textiles, iron and steel) were at the heart of economic growth. Between 1850 and 1875, annual coal production rose from 49.4 million tons to 131.9 million tons. Export of cotton textiles increased from an annual average of 978 million yards in the 1840s to 3573 million yards in the 1870s. This economic boom not only benefitted the business community but also the domestic workforce. The following table illustrates the rising prosperity that went beyond 1873.

Base Year: 1850 = 100

	Money wages	Real wages
1850	100	100
1855	116	94
1860	114	105
1866	132	117
1871	137	125
1874	155	136

Another indicator of the growing prosperity in the mid-nineteenth century was the increase in the workforce in staple industries. For example, in 1850, there were 191,000 cotton spinners and 216,000 coal miners. By 1873, these figures had risen to 230,000 and 465,000 respectively. Between 1850 and 1870, the value of imports increased from £103 million to £303 million. Exports went from £83 million to £244 million in the same period. This clearly reveals a **balance of payments deficit**. This was offset by invisible earnings such as shipping, insurance and banking. The deficit underlines Britain's growth as a consumer nation in the mid-nineteenth century.

There was no doubt that Britain was the world's leading trading nation. The nature of the imports reveals some important evidence that helps to explain why economic prosperity was so closely linked to foreign and imperial policy. By 1870, 27 per cent of the total value of imports was accounted for by textile raw materials, while foodstuffs accounted for a further 34 per cent of the total value of imports. These figures indicate the expansion of British industry and job creation. They also underline the increased consumption of food across the whole population. British foreign and imperial policy had to protect trade because businessmen and entrepreneurs were prospering and the general population demanded a share in the benefits of prosperity through increased consumption.

EXPANSION OF THE EMPIRE

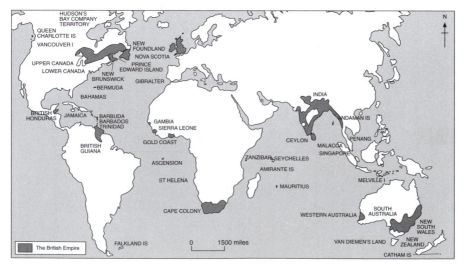

The extent of the British Empire in 1850

In the last quarter of the nineteenth century, Britain adopted a more expansionist view of **imperialism**. The British Empire up to this point had been a source of profitable markets for British manufactured goods and a provider of cheap raw materials. The expansion of the empire became a guiding principle of British imperial policy after 1885. The key question is why did this development in policy occur?

- Economic imperialism – One commonly held explanation for imperial growth is that Britain needed to develop new markets for its manufactured goods. Trade patterns in the last quarter of the nineteenth century were changing. The European markets were becoming saturated, and demand for British manufactured goods was in decline. One reason for this shift was the fact that Europe was experiencing its own industrialisation and was therefore becoming self-sufficient and less dependent upon British imports. An expanded empire presented new opportunities to offset the decline in Britain's European export market. Furthermore, protectionism in the USA, France and Germany limited Britain's access to markets in these countries. Another factor lies in the influence of British industrialists, manufacturers and investors over government policy. Some historians have argued that there was a **surplus of investment capital** in Britain.

The economic wealth of Britain was not generated solely through manufacturing. Invisible earnings were a major contributor, particularly in reducing the balance of payments deficit. An expanding empire offered new opportunities for investment.

- Strategic imperialism – In order to protect existing trade routes, particularly to India, and the development of new routes for imperial trade, it was necessary for the British navy to strengthen its strategic power on a global scale. In effect, this meant having more territorial bases. It meant having a larger empire. In addition to this, it was clear that by the 1870s that the industrialisation and economic expansion of the USA and Europe had not only weakened Britain's hitherto unrivalled economic power, but also heightened competition amongst nations with increasingly comparable economic strength. Britain's answer was to protect its position by expanding its empire in order to extend its strategic power.

From the 1870s not only was Britain's economic power under threat, particularly from the USA and Germany, but also its status as a great power. If other states began to increase their territorial power then so must Britain. Empire was increasingly becoming a measure of international power. International rivalry and the race for power stimulated imperial expansion.

- Cultural imperialism – This is the idea that Britain wanted to bring 'civilisation' to those parts of the world as yet 'uncivilised'. For the British, civilisation meant British culture and this meant educating the indigenous peoples to accept the notion of European superiority and, therefore, the logic of their own inferiority. Cultural imperialism may be seen as an outcome of imperialism rather than as a primary motive for imperial expansion. By attempting to westernise the values and culture of the local populations, Britain sought to secure its control more effectively.

- Social imperialism – Success in expanding Britain's power base had vote winning potential at home. The Conservative Party under Disraeli and Lord Salisbury exploited this phenomenon as British influence in Africa grew. The electorate was expanding as a result of the Parliamentary Reform Acts of 1867 and 1884. Patriotism was becoming a popular concept and successive governments were able to use imperial expansionism to generate patriotism and increase their own popularity amongst the voters.

WHY DID BRITAIN FEAR RUSSIA?

In part, Britain's priorities were founded upon preserving the European balance of power and protecting its own international trade, particularly with India. The greatest perceived threat to these objectives was Russia. Russia was regarded as:

- Expansionist – The aim of Russian foreign policy was seen as a desire to expand westwards into Europe. This would be achieved by exploiting the weaknesses of the Turkish Empire.

KEY PEOPLE

Viscount Palmerston (1774–1865) Palmerston entered Parliament in 1807. In 1830, he joined the Whigs. His popular image was that, primarily, of an aggressive patriot who single-mindedly pursued Britain's interests. Palmerston reminded Parliament that every Briton 'shall feel confident that the watchful eye and the strong arm of England will protect him against injustice and wrong'. However, there are many examples of caution, diplomatic subtly and practical flexibility in his actions, particularly during the revolts in Europe in 1848 and the moves towards the unification of Italy. He was Foreign Secretary between 1846 and 1851 and Prime Minister from 1855–8 and 1859–65. He died soon after winning the 1865 general election.

Louis Philippe (1773-1850) King of France between 1830 and 1848. He was the eldest son of the Duc d'Orleans. Upon the abdication of Charles X in 1830, he was elected lieutenant-general of the kingdom. In July he became King. In 1848, he was overthrown and escaped to England.

Louis Napoleon (1808-73) He was the nephew of Napoleon. In 1848 he was elected President of France and with popular support he was proclaimed Emperor Napoleon III and head of the Second Empire in 1852. Following the defeat of France at the hands of the Prussians in 1870 he abdicated.

- Aggressive – Russia was seen as being willing to use aggressive diplomacy and military force to achieve its objective of westward expansion.

This image of Russia underpinned British foreign policy thinking from the 1840s. The Turkish Empire and Eastern Europe were seen as the key to Britain's ability to protect its own interests. Any expansion or exploitation of instability or weakness in these regions would threaten Britain's influence in the Mediterranean and ultimately its trade routes to India. By the turn of the century Britain became more inclined to cooperate with the Russians. The view was that the Russian threat to India had declined. India not only had a huge population, it also provided cheap, essential commodities such as tea. It was a lucrative market for British manufactured goods and it gave Britain incomparable levels of international prestige. It was, by the 1870s, 'the jewel in the imperial crown'. This was amply illustrated when, in 1876, Disraeli persuaded Parliament to grant Queen Victoria the title Empress of India. This reinforced the link between imperialism and patriotism, a link that was to become increasingly significant after 1880.

Were the principles put into practice?

Viscount Palmerston may be regarded as the first in a series of influential figures who shaped British foreign and imperial policy in the second half of the nineteenth century. An examination of the key events will illustrate the nature of this contribution.

THE REVOLTS IN EUROPE, 1848

France

In February 1848, the reign of **Louis Philippe** was brought to a sudden end. Initially he was replaced by a radical government and then, finally, in July 1848, by the election of **Louis Napoleon** Bonaparte as President. France had become a republic.

Palmerston offered Louis Philippe no support but he did support Louis Napoleon. Palmerston backed Louis Napoleon, not because he favoured republicanism and democracy, but because he wanted a stable government in France with which he could do business. A republic in

France meant order, and order greatly reduced the threat to the preservation of the balance of power.

Austria

Palmerston showed no sympathy for the liberal movements in Austria. In March 1848, rebellion flared up across the Austrian Empire. The critical issue for Britain was the maintenance of the Austrian Empire, or at the very least its preservation to a point at which it was able to continue its role as a barrier to possible Russian expansion. Disorder in the empire could herald the disintegration of European stability.

Palmerston urged Austria to consolidate its empire by withdrawing from its Italian possessions following the revolts in Venice and Lombardy. Palmerstonian pragmatism was clearly at work here. In Palmerston's view, a reduced but stronger Austrian Empire was preferable to a larger weak empire, particularly when the Turkish Empire was also facing serious weaknesses which might open up opportunities for expansion to the Russians. Austrian imperialists responded quickly. The revolts amongst the Czechs were crushed, the constitutional government in Vienna was overthrown, and Venice and Lombardy were restored under direct Austrian rule. Austria then sought Russia's help in crushing the revolts in Hungary. Up to this point Palmerston was content, but the inclusion of Russia in the events forced him to condemn Austria's treatment of the Hungarians. He appeared to be the defender of liberals and revolutionaries. Reality was quite different. It was the presence of Russian troops in Hungary and an apparent Russo–Austrian alliance that alarmed Palmerston. The twin fears of Russian expansionism and threats to the balance of power motivated Palmerston's action, not the desire to protect democracy in Hungary or, indeed, anywhere else.

THE DON PACIFICO INCIDENT, 1850

Don Pacifico was a Portuguese Jew who had been born in the British colony of Gibraltar. After his property had been damaged in Athens in 1847, he demanded compensation from the Greek government. Palmerston supported Don Pacifico and sent gunboats to Athens and seized a number of Greek ships. Don Pacifico received his compensation.

This affair shows no real consistency with the aims of British foreign policy. It offended Austria, Russia and France. All these states had guaranteed Greek independence for which Britain had shown such little regard. It merely served to add to Palmerston's reputation as a bully of small nations. It was a blatant piece of **aggressive patriotism** and had more to do with Palmerston's political popularity than British foreign policy priorities.

THE SECOND ANGLO–CHINESE WAR, 1856–60

In 1856, the *Arrow*, sailing under a British flag, was seized by the Chinese. They accused its crew of acts of piracy. The British Consul in Canton demanded the ship's release and an official apology. When China refused, Palmerston supported the decision to bomb Canton. With French support, British troops went on to assault Peking in 1860. It was at this point that the Chinese had no option other than to submit to British demands. The outcome led to an expansion of trade with China as more Chinese ports were opened up to international trade. Britain also received a guarantee of access to the Chinese interior.

Palmerston had protected British interests. He had expanded Britain's international trade and the British economy benefitted. British international prestige was enhanced. The aggressive pursuit of Britain's national interests was possible in the Far East because it did not threaten European stability or British interests in Europe.

ITALIAN UNIFICATION, 1859–60

Palmerston regarded Italian nationalists and liberals as a block on the more radical groups who might threaten British commercial and strategic interests in the Mediterranean if they were to come to power. He also saw an Austrian presence in Italy as a restraining influence against French expansionism there.

However, when Piedmont invaded Austrian territory in northern Italy, Palmerston backed the Piedmontese. In 1860, **Garibaldi** invaded Sicily. The British navy helped Garibaldi not only to reach Sicily but also Naples. This was a vital step in the creation of the independent sovereign state of Italy. Palmerston's priority was to support Italian unification to enable Austria to consolidate its own position

---

KEY THEME

Aggressive patriotism This is the idea that any level of force is acceptable to protect Britain's national interests. For Palmerston, patriotism was about promoting Britain's image as a country that was to be respected and this would be achieved by threats and direct action if necessary.

KEY PERSON

Giuseppe Garibaldi (1807-82) Italian patriot who joined the Young Italy movement in 1834. In 1859 he took his 'thousand' volunteers to help Mazzini's rebels free Sicily. He made a major contribution to the creation of the Kingdom of Italy.

What principles guided Britain's foreign and imperial policies between 1846 and 1902? 13

in the rest of its territories without Italy being an additional burden. Austria was an essential element in Palmerston's determination to maintain stability in Europe. French influence in Italy was limited as Britain basked in the support of a grateful Italy. Trade with Italy increased and Britain had a strategically important ally in the Mediterranean.

The incident illustrates Palmerston's commitment to preserving the balance of power in Europe. An expansion of French power had been prevented. Austria could continue to play its role without too many problems caused by the loss of Italian lands. British interests in the Mediterranean had been protected and enhanced.

FOREIGN AND IMPERIAL POLICY FROM 1865

William Gladstone's first administration began in 1868 and ended in 1874. By 1871, Prussia had defeated France and created a new, united Germany in Europe. Germany was rapidly moving towards becoming the dominant great power in continental Europe. Germany's European strategy became focused on diplomatically isolating France in order to enhance Germany's power base.

In imperial affairs, an important change had taken place in 1867. The British North America Act gave Canada internal self-government. This signalled a shift towards granting Britain's other **white dominions** similar status.

India was exposed to a growing threat after Russia conquered territories close by in central Asia. The conquest of Samarkhand, Khiva and Bokhara opened up India's northwest frontier to Russian aggression. Protecting India became a priority of British imperial policy after 1870.

During his first ministry, Gladstone wanted to break with what he regarded as Palmerstonian 'sabre rattling' and the aggressive foreign policy that seemed to characterise it. He wanted to raise the conduct of British foreign policy to a higher moral level. He was strongly criticised for rejecting **interventionism** and promoting the rights of nations. To many, this appeared to be disregarding the interests of Britain. The question is, is this a valid interpretation of Gladstone's policies and does it suggest a break with continuity?

KEY PERSON

William Ewart Gladstone (1809–98) Gladstone was born into a wealthy Liverpool merchant's family. In 1832, he was elected Tory MP for Newark. He was Chancellor of the Exchequer between 1853 and 1855, and subsequently joined the Liberal Party and served as Chancellor from 1859–66. Between 1868 and 1894, he was Prime Minister on four occasions. In terms of foreign and imperial policy, he was committed to the Concert of Europe. He favoured peace not war and believed that diplomacy and arbitration were at all times preferable to fighting. He was convinced that Britain had a responsibility to rule its empire but was not committed to defend the colonies' internal security when they attained self-governing status.

KEY TERMS

White dominions Those parts of the British Empire which were colonised by white people who assumed control and did not include the native population in decision-making. Such colonies included New Zealand, Australia, Cape Colony and Canada. Non-dominion colonies were completely ruled by Britain and its representatives in the colony.

Interventionism States will take action in the affairs of another country if such action appears to strengthen or protect their own interests.

THE FRANCO–PRUSSIAN WAR, 1870–1

Gladstone's inaction was consistent with his commitment to non-interventionism, but it made no contribution to preserving the European balance of power. A significant redirection of policy had taken place as Britain allowed Germany to emerge as the focal point of European diplomacy. It was not simply a question of one great power, France, being replaced by a successor, Germany. Economically and militarily, Germany posed a far greater threat to the balance of power because it had the capacity and the ambition to become ever stronger.

Prussia's victory over France heralded the transformation of the balance of power in Europe. This was a serious external crisis for Britain. Gladstone took no action beyond securing a commitment from Prussia and France to jointly respect Belgian neutrality.

THE REVOCATION OF THE BLACK SEA CLAUSES OF THE TREATY OF PARIS

The Treaty of Paris, which had ended the Crimean War, had banned Russia from maintaining a naval fleet on the Black Sea. The potential danger of a Russian fleet in the Black Sea had been a major reason for Britain's involvement in the war. Gladstone convened a Great Power Conference. Once again, Gladstone had avoided war but he had also abandoned Britain's policy of controlling Russian expansionism. He clung to the idea that the Concert of Europe was intact and could be used effectively to preserve peace.

KEY EVENT

The American Civil War, 1861-65 A war between states from the north and south of the country. The dispute arose primarily as a result of disagreements over the right of states to choose whether or not they retained slavery. The southern states were prepared to leave the union of states that united America over this issue. The war ended with defeat for the south.

THE ALABAMA AWARD, 1872

The USA repeated its claims for compensation for damage caused by the *Alabama*, a warship built in Britain for the South during **the American Civil War**. During the war, the *Alabama* had contributed to the capture or sinking of up to 57 Northern vessels. Unlike Palmerston, who had simply rejected such claims, Gladstone agreed to an international conference at Geneva. This awarded the USA £3.25 million in damages and Gladstone agreed to pay.

The incident illustrates his commitment to the collective will of international opinion in contrast to the

Palmerstonian approach. Many saw this as a blow to British international prestige, although it did ensure Britain remained on good terms with the USA. It suggested that international cooperation was successful at a relatively small price.

IMPERIAL AFFAIRS, 1868–74

Gladstone implemented a series of actions that appeared to suggest that he was not an imperialist and was therefore breaking faith with traditional policy.

- He withdrew British troops from Canada and New Zealand at a time when these colonies faced internal revolt.
- He offered the pro-independence Canadian Prime Minister, **Alexander Galt**, a knighthood.
- In 1872, Cape Colony was granted self-government.

However, Gladstone was not seeking to dismantle the empire. He believed that the 'white' colonies should be self-governing but still closely linked to Britain. The rest, including India, would be ruled directly by Britain. In this way, Gladstone was consistent with his predecessors' commitment to the centrality of India at the heart of Britain's imperial power.

Benjamin Disraeli, Gladstone's life-long political rival, was committed to the empire but he had no definite plans for its expansion. He believed that the empire was a measure and an expression of Britain's power. The maintenance of this power over India was central to his thinking, to the point where he added the description 'Empress of India' to Queen Victoria's titles in 1876. This served to link the monarchy with the empire and to bind India more closely than ever before to Britain.

IMPERIAL AFFAIRS, 1874–80

The Suez Canal Shares, 1875

Disraeli started Britain's involvement in Egypt through his purchase of shares in the Suez Canal. Disraeli secretly used a £4 million loan from **the Rothschild family** to purchase a 44 per cent share in the canal. This decision turned out to be of vital importance in the development of British influence in Africa and it was an essential development in

KEY PEOPLE

Alexander Galt (1817-93) Originally from England he moved to Canada in 1835 and became a member of the Canadian Parliament in 1849. Along with other posts, he was Canadian High Commissioner in Britain between 1880 and 1883.

Benjamin Disraeli (1804–81) Disraeli was born into a wealthy Jewish family, although in 1817 he was baptised into the Anglican Church. He was elected as MP for Maidstone in 1837. After attacking Peel over the Corn Laws, he rose to become leader of the Conservative Party in the House of Commons in 1848. He became a life-long political rival of Gladstone and this was fully reflected in the very different approaches the two men took towards foreign policy. He became an unrivalled favourite of Queen Victoria and in 1876 she elevated him to the title of Earl of Beaconsfield. He was Prime Minister in 1868 and between 1874 and 1880. He died in 1881.

The Rothschild family A wealthy family whose riches were based on the banking dynasty founded by Meyer Rothschild (1743–1812).

A cartoon published in 1876 in the magazine Punch. The caption reads 'The Lion's Share. Take care anyone who touches it!'

THE LION'S SHARE.
"GARE À QUI LA TOUCHE !"

KEY PERSON

Lord Lytton (1831-91)
A statesman and a diplomat who, in addition to being Viceroy of India between 1876 and 1880, was British Ambassador in Paris in 1887. He was also a poet and a novelist.

KEY EVENT

The Battle of Isandlwana, 1879 A humiliating defeat for the British, when almost 1200 troops were massacred by poorly armed Zulu warriors.

KEY PERSON

Sir Bartle Frere (1815-84)
Primarily associated with India, he was appointed High Commissioner for South Africa in 1877. He was a keen defender of British imperial interests. His decision to make a pre-emptive strike against the Zulus in 1878, and thereby strengthen British control, was prompted largely by a fear of a Russian attack on South Africa brought on by events in Europe and the Balkans in 1878.

the protection of the route to India. Strategically and commercially, the canal was vital to British interests, not only in the Mediterranean but also in India, the Far East and Austral–Asia.

The Afghan Wars, 1878 and 1879

Afghanistan was seen as the route that Russia might have used to threaten India. Therefore, by controlling Afghanistan, Britain could strengthen Indian security. Once again, the protection of India figured largely in British policy. The decision to install a pro-British ruler in Afghanistan made by the India Secretary, Lord Cranbrook, and the Viceroy of India, **Lord Lytton**, proved disastrous. British troops were involved in two futile campaigns, which only served to humiliate Britain and weaken its international prestige.

The Zulu War, 1878

An equally humiliating defeat was experienced by Britain at the hands of the Zulus at **the Battle of Isandlwana**. Once again, a British official, **Sir Bartle Frere**, the High Commissioner of South Africa, had taken an initiative that went seriously wrong. Rather than being a reckless imperialist, Disraeli may be seen as the victim of the recklessness of others. His weakness lies in the fact that he did nothing to stop the dangerous actions of others.

The 'Eastern Question', 1875–8

A decaying Turkish Empire appeared to open up opportunities for Russian expansionism southwards. Disraeli was convinced that this would ultimately threaten the Suez Canal and therefore the security of the route for Indian and British commerce. The defence of Britain's trade and international prestige were central to Disraeli's objectives in terms of his reaction to the 'fate' of the Turkish Empire. These objectives were totally consistent with longstanding British foreign policy objectives.

When Russia threatened Constantinople, Disraeli moved troops from India to Malta, called up reservists and placed Britain into a state of war readiness. Avoiding war at all costs was clearly not at the top of Disraeli's agenda. Ultimately, the Congress of Berlin in 1878 was, in many respects, a triumph for Disraeli's approach. Russia was forced to abandon many of its gains and Britain's position in the Mediterranean was strengthened through the acquisition of Cyprus. The European balance of power had been preserved.

GLADSTONE'S SECOND ADMINISTRATION, 1880–5

Gladstone favoured the consolidation of the empire, partly by reducing its size and through the development of self-governing colonies. Ironically, it was during this administration that the empire expanded in size.

The First Boer War, 1880–1

The Dutch Boer settlers of **the Transvaal** demanded their independence from British rule. The government feared that this might become a general armed revolt throughout South Africa.

In 1881, a British force was destroyed at **the Battle of Majuba Hill**. True to his anti-imperialist stance, Gladstone convened **the Pretoria Convention**. This was a classic example of Gladstone's willingness to assume some of the responsibility of a colony without having real control over it.

KEY TERM

The 'Eastern Question' A term based on the certainty that the Turkish Empire was in a state of terminal decline. Its collapse raised the issue of what would happen to the future stability of Europe in terms of the creation of new states and the possible expansionist opportunities open to Russia.

KEY PLACE

The Transvaal Britain assumed control of this Boer territory in 1877. This became part of Britain's expanding territory in South Africa.

KEY EVENTS

The Battle of Majuba Hill, 1881 The Boers declared their independence and defeated a small British force at Majuba Hill in Natal. This was a major Boer victory against Britain's military presence.

The Pretoria Convention, 1881 This came about as a result of the Boer revolt in 1881. The Transvaal was granted internal self-government, but Britain retained control over Transvaal's foreign policy.

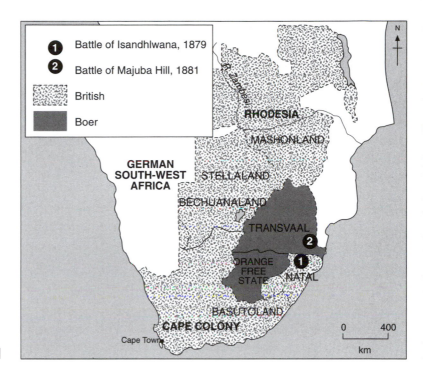

British expansion in South Africa by 1881

Egypt, 1882

Egypt was part of the Turkish Empire when nationalist revolts erupted in 1882. Gladstone accepted that it was essential that British financial investments in Egypt and the Suez Canal zone were protected. He wanted a joint Anglo–French invasion force to intervene and restore stability. This was totally consistent with his concept of international cooperation. The strategy failed and a purely British force carried out the action. Gladstone anticipated only a brief occupation, but Britain remained in control of Egypt until 1922. Almost inadvertently, Gladstone had expanded the empire and taken a hugely significant step in protecting the security of the Suez Canal and the route to India. Furthermore, he had succeeded in promoting economic opportunities for British manufacturers. Egypt was a major producer of raw cotton, which British textile manufacturers were anxious to exploit. Egypt was also a potentially huge market for the importation of British technology, particularly railway transport technology.

The Sudan, 1883–5

The Sudan was an Egyptian possession. A rebellion led by **Mohammed Ahmad** (the Mahdi) erupted and in 1883 his

KEY PERSON

Mohammed Ahmad (1844-85) Also known as the Mahdi or Muslim messiah. A Sudanese, who in 1881 declared that his divine mission was to purify Islam and the governments that defiled it. He rebelled against Egyptian rule in the Sudan. In 1885, his forces seized Khartoum and killed General Gordon.

followers destroyed a British led Egyptian force sent to end the rebellion. Gladstone sent **General Gordon** to the Sudan with orders only to evacuate British and Egyptian nationals. Gordon disobeyed his orders and installed himself in the Sudanese capital, Khartoum, intending to await relief and establish British control of the Sudan. Gladstone delayed making a final decision about the relief and Gordon's force was slaughtered two days before a British force under General Wolsey arrived.

Gladstone was condemned by the public and politicians alike. His anti-imperialism had gone too far and he lost the 1885 general election.

Although very different, there were some significant similarities between Gladstone and Disraeli. Perhaps the most significant was that neither man strongly supported the idea of an expanding empire for Britain. The protection of India and the routes to it was another common thread that united the two adversaries. Gladstone's concept of foreign policy as a moral process was less similar to Disraeli's thinking.

LORD SALISBURY, 1885, 1886–92, 1895–1901

Lord Salisbury was driven broadly by the same objectives that had motivated his predecessors since 1846. His aim was to protect the British Empire, one of the cornerstones of Britain's economic wealth and global power, and maintain a balance of power in Europe, the guarantee of stability and peace for Britain. Salisbury saw Russia and France as the primary threats to the fulfilment of his aims. He recognised the role of Germany as a major contributor to European stability and believed that Germany could be used to offset the ambitions of France and Russia.

What was Salisbury's European policy in 1886–92?

Anglo–French tensions had been heightened since 1882 when Britain took over control of Egypt. This had undermined French influence in North Africa. The issue of Russian expansionist ambitions in the Near East and in the states neighbouring India remained an on-going problem for Britain. Salisbury's strategy was to establish closer links with the powers of the **Triple Alliance**.

KEY PEOPLE

General Charles George Gordon (1833-85)
Gordon was a career soldier who fought in the Crimean War. In 1860 he crushed a rebellion in China and became known as Chinese Gordon. He was appointed Governor of the Sudan in 1877, but resigned in 1880. He was killed at Khartoum two days before a relief column arrived to raise the ten month siege by the Mahdi's forces.

Lord Salisbury (1830–1903) Robert Arthur Cecil succeeded his brother as Viscount Cranborne in 1865 and his father as third Marquis of Salisbury in 1868. He was a Conservative and became the last British Prime Minister in the House of Lords. He is most often associated with isolating Britain from foreign alliances, but the exact nature of this is a matter of debate. He was not convinced that control of Constantinople was the basis of Russia's threat to India. However, the safety of the Mediterranean route to the East was of supreme importance to him and Egypt was to assume unparalleled significance in British foreign and imperial policy under Salisbury.

KEY ALLIANCE

Triple Alliance, 1882 This was a military alliance between Germany, Austria and Italy. Essentially, it was an anti-France and anti-Russian alliance system, which had been brokered by Germany.

KEY AGREEMENTS

The Mediterranean Agreements, 1887 The first agreement was with Italy. Italy was bitterly resentful of France's takeover of Tunis in 1881. Italy and Britain jointly agreed to prevent the growth of French influence in North Africa. The second agreement included Austria and was designed to protect the status quo in the Balkans and the Straits. The agreement was primarily anti-Russian.

KEY TERM

Two-power standard
Britain's fleet was to be as large as the combined fleets of its two main rivals. This would give Britain a margin of naval superiority.

KEY EVENT

Turkish massacres of Armenians, 1895 Armenia was a Turkish province fringing the Russian Empire. The Turks were determined to crush any aspirations of independence amongst the two million Christians living there. It was this that led to the widespread slaughter of Armenian Christians. Divisions amongst the great powers enabled the Turks to get away with the massacres because there was minimal international reaction.

Salisbury did not seek to join the alliance system because he did not wish to commit Britain to a European entanglement, but equally he did not want Britain to face dangerous isolation in Europe. The agreements he made in 1887 illustrated this approach to foreign policy and how he sought to protect British interests without a formal commitment to the Triple Alliance powers. Salisbury's style was aimed at preserving flexibility.

Two secret agreements were made in 1887 called **the Mediterranean Agreements**. Although Salisbury, in 1889, identified France as a potential threat, he refused Germany's offer of a defensive alliance directed against the French. This was because it would have committed Britain to back Germany's anti-French tactics but it would not have ensured German support for Britain against possible Russian aggression against India. Once again, Salisbury chose to build flexibility into his foreign policy by deliberately avoiding any firm ties based on treaties, however relevant they appeared to be to British interests. His alternative approach was to expand Britain's naval power so that it maintained the **two-power standard**. This underlines Salisbury's commitment to protecting the empire and therefore the priority he gave to the empire.

What were Salisbury's policies outside Europe in 1895–1901?

The Balkans

Britain's traditionally anti-Russian position was compromised by Salisbury from 1895. In 1895, **Turkish massacres of Armenians** living in eastern Turkey created a crisis which the Russians could have easily exploited and intervened in the Turkish Empire. Austria demanded that Britain make a binding commitment to defend Constantinople against Russian aggression. To the Austrians, this was perfectly consistent with the 1887 agreement. For Salisbury, it was an impossible situation. Binding agreements were simply not part of his political and diplomatic vocabulary. The outcome was that Britain's links with the Triple Alliance were severed and Britain's isolation from European diplomacy was deepened. This was a profound shift from the position of influence Britain had maintained prior to Salisbury's administrations.

Egypt

The immediate effect of Salisbury's withdrawal from Constantinople was to increase the importance of Britain's occupation of Egypt. This state was crucial in protecting Britain's sea route to India. The defence against the Russian threat had shifted from Constantinople into the Eastern Mediterranean. This shift in strategic thinking was a break with the traditional policy of containing Russian expansionism. It also meant that British security in Egypt became a priority. To reinforce this, Salisbury accepted that the Sudan should be conquered. The Sudan controlled the upper reaches of the River Nile and the Nile was vital to Egypt's economic development.

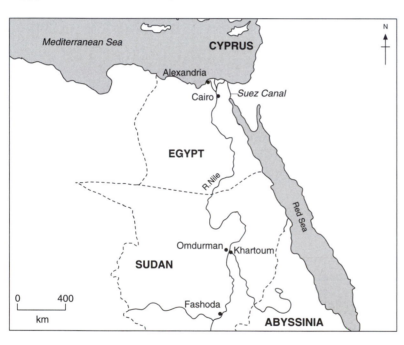

Egypt and the Sudan, 1898

In 1898, **General Kitchener** defeated a Sudanese army at Omdurman. This force was then ordered to stand firm against a rival French expedition in the region. This Anglo–French encounter took place at Fashoda, and the French withdrew. This incident confirmed British supremacy over the whole of Egypt and the Sudan but it undermined Anglo–French relations. Britain's European isolationism deepened.

The Far East

The Chinese Empire was in a state of terminal decay. Britain had already established a significant trading interest along the Yangtze Valley up to the port of Shanghai. British policy had been based on an **open door approach** to other European powers.

Germany and Russia were promoting their interests in China. Russian expansionism in the Far East continued through the penetration into the Chinese province of Manchuria. Despite the efforts of the Colonial Secretary, **Joseph Chamberlain**, Britain failed to draw Germany into an anti-Russian alliance designed to curb Russian ambitions in the Far East.

DID SALISBURY'S FOREIGN POLICY PUT BRITAIN INTO A SITUATION OF 'SPLENDID ISOLATION'?

In February 1896, the First Lord of the Admiralty, Lord Goschen, said:

> *Our situation is not an isolation of weakness; it is deliberately chosen, this freedom, to act as we choose in any circumstances that might arise.*

By 1895, Britain was the only European power not attached to a formal alliance in Europe. By 1893 France had freed itself from its international isolation through its alliance with Russia. Even by 1898 there was great hostility between Britain and France, particularly over the Fashoda incident. It was Germany's move towards naval rivalry and support for the Boers that pushed Britain into a more conciliatory relationship with France by the turn of the century.

Salisbury was, like many of his predecessors, determined not to entangle Britain in war. Alliance commitments could easily lead to war. Prudence rather than pure isolationism

PARTNERS.

BRITANNIA. "AFTER ALL, MY DEAR, WE NEEDN'T TROUBLE OURSELVES ABOUT THE OTHERS."
COLONIA. "NO; WE CAN ALWAYS DANCE TOGETHER, YOU AND I!"

A cartoon entitled 'Partners' published in 1901 in the magazine Punch

characterised Salisbury's foreign policies. The evidence as to a lack of alliances is clear. Primarily, isolationism was a deliberate policy designed not merely to place Britain outside Europe and focus entirely on imperial issues, but also to ensure Britain's freedom of action in international relations. Britain also wanted to avoid conflict, which they may not be able either to sustain or control.

Overall, there was a consistency in British foreign and imperial policy between 1846 and 1902.

- Russia was perceived as a threat and British governments never wavered from this view.
- Imperial trade had to be protected, as had the routes that enabled that trade to flourish.
- European peace, based on a balance of power, and the avoidance of European war were central themes in policy-making throughout the period.
- There was a remarkable degree of continuity of purpose in the principles that guided policy. It was the methods used to fulfil the principles that proved to be so variable in consistency.

SUMMARY QUESTIONS

1 Explain the importance of **two** of the principles that guided British foreign and imperial policy between 1846 and 1902.

2 Why were relations with Russia so central to British foreign policy from 1846?

3 Explain how and with what success British foreign and imperial interests were protected by political leaders up to 1902.

4 Assess the reasons why British foreign and imperial policies between 1846 and 1902 were consistently maintained.

KEY CONCEPT

Splendid isolation An idea with a number of interpretations. Essentially it suggests that Britain chose to rely upon its own strength, particularly through its imperial power, rather than commit itself to European alliance systems. Alternatively, there is the view that Britain had no choice. It was frozen out of European alliance systems by the other great European powers.

CHAPTER 2

Why did Britain go to war with Russia in the Crimea between 1854 and 1856?

Britain's involvement in the Crimean War was partly the result of a weak and indecisive government under Lord Aberdeen, clumsy diplomacy, and the effects of a growing tide of **Russophobia** both within the government and amongst the general public.

Also, for Britain, the war was seen as essentially a preventative war. The aim was to prevent:

- disruption to the European balance of power
- Britain's naval dominance in the Mediterranean from being challenged
- threats to the security of the route to India
- the break-up of the Turkish Empire.

The target of all these preventative aims was Russia. We have to ask whether or not Britain had clearly identified the major threat to its own interests and the stability of Europe or whether Britain was simply drawn into an unnecessary war through the chaotic diplomacy of France and Russia and its own irrational fear of Russian actions.

WHAT WAS THE EUROPEAN BALANCE OF POWER?

The map of Europe in 1854 was largely the same as it had been in 1815. European stability had been successfully preserved since **the Congress of Vienna**, but, in 1848, revolts broke out in France, Austria, Italy and the German states. For Britain, a country committed to the preservation of the balance of power in Europe, these developments were dangerous. For example, any threat to the unity and order of the Austrian Empire might have reduced Austria's effectiveness as a barrier to Russian expansionism westwards into Europe. Indeed, the rise of **nationalism** within the Austrian Empire could have reinforced the nationalist sentiments that were already becoming a problem in the Turkish Empire. This would further weaken its structure and open up the way for even greater

KEY TERM

Russophobia Essentially, it was an irrational dislike and fear of the Russians. Palmerston was a powerful supporter of this idea. Russia was presented by Russophobes as a constant threat to British interests. Anything Russian was to be despised and viewed with extreme suspicion.

KEY EVENT

The Congress of Vienna, 1814-15 After the defeat of Napoleon Bonaparte, an international conference was held in Vienna. Its aim was to create a balance of power amongst the powers of Europe in order to prevent future European wars.

KEY CONCEPT

Nationalism The idea that people with a shared linguistic, cultural and religious identity should come together as one nation. These shared characteristics demand that the people are not part of an empire or ruled by a foreign power.

expansionist opportunities for the Russians who were beginning to revive their support for pro-nationalist Christians within the Turkish Empire.

The most straightforward way to preserve the balance of power from about 1850 was to ensure that the existing territorial order remained intact. It was the weakness of the Turkish Empire and the assumption that it was inevitable that Russia would seek to exploit this and expand into the Turkish Empire that convinced some British political leaders, such as Palmerston, that Russia posed a threat to the security of the balance of power in Europe.

What was the significance of the condition of the Turkish Empire?

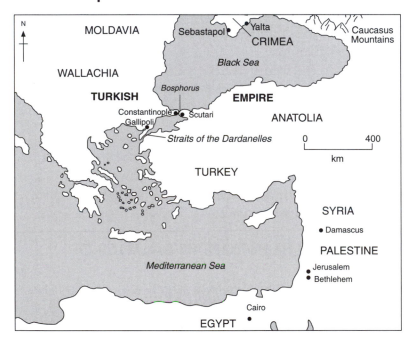

The Crimean War, 1854–6

By 1850, the Turkish Empire appeared to be on the brink of terminal decline. Major religious divisions had weakened imperial unity and the Turks had made few concessions or gestures towards any form of religious or ethnic tolerance. Should the empire collapse, what form of power base would replace it in South Eastern Europe? The possible alternatives included:

- a series of independent states freed from Turkish control and not committed to the Concert of Europe

- independent states, some allied to Russia, some to Austria or another European power
- the splitting of the empire in Europe and its division between Russia and Austria.

Each of these alternatives threatened the balance of power in Europe. Austria feared the emergence of independent states on its frontiers. Nationalism could spread into the Austrian Empire. A vast amount of Austrian trade passed along the River Danube and this could be placed in serious danger if the status quo shifted. Russian influence in the Mediterranean could increase and this would threaten British trading interests there and the overland route to India, which was the most economically lucrative part of the British Empire.

BRITAIN, THE MEDITERRANEAN AND INDIA

The Crimean War may be regarded as a war motivated by British imperialism, as well as by fear of upsetting the balance of power in Europe. The possibility of Russian expansionism was translated by some into Russian control of Constantinople and **the Straits**. This would give Russia unrestricted naval access to the Mediterranean and the Near East.

A Russian fleet in the Mediterranean would have undermined British naval supremacy there. In turn, this loss of dominance would have weakened Britain's influence in the Middle East and thereby created an indirect threat to the security of the route to India.

India was Britain's largest colony. The trade monopoly held by **the East India Company** had ended in 1813. Since then, independent commerce had increased to the point where India held premier place in British colonial trade. Indian jute and tea were essential imports into Britain, and India itself represented a major market for British engineering technology and financial investment in the development of railways. **The Great Exhibition** of 1851, held in London, underlined the vast potential that India had for British entrepreneurs.

KEY PLACE

The Straits This sea route linked the Black Sea to the Mediterranean. It was the route through the Dardanelles and the Bosphorous. The area was controlled by Constantinople.

KEY ORGANISATION

The East India Company Founded in 1600, it became a powerful trading organisation. It was important in establishing a British presence in India where it, amongst other things, set up the cultivation of tea.

KEY EVENT

The Great Exhibition, 1851 A purpose designed structure, the Crystal Palace, was built to house this exhibition of British industrial and technological achievements. It was designed, partly, to demonstrate Britain's industrial might. Exhibits from across the Empire were also on display.

WHAT WAS THE ROLE OF THE FRENCH, THE RUSSIANS AND THE TURKS?

The French

In 1848, Louis Napoleon became President of France. The restoration of France's influence in Europe was a priority for Louis Napoleon. The way this objective was to be achieved was through challenging Russia, the country most determined to limit France's aspirations of restoring its international prestige. The opportunity to do this presented itself in 1850.

The Holy Places dispute arose over the guardianship of the Holy Places in Palestine. At the heart of the quarrel was the question of whose influence, that of France or Russia, would be established at Constantinople. The affair opened up a series of attractive opportunities for Louis Napoleon:

- success would reinforce Catholic support for him in France
- it could drive a wedge between Roman Catholic Austria and Orthodox Christian Russia and so weaken any alliance they may form against France
- it could strengthen French influence over the Turks by excluding the Russians
- it could enhance France's international status and prestige.

France demanded that the Turks restore the rights of French Catholic monks to supervise the holy sites. **Tsar Nicolas I**'s international prestige was at stake and, equally serious, the influence that Russia may have over the Turks. In December 1852, the **Sultan, Abd-ul-Medjid**, gave in to French demands. His decision had been influenced by the fact that the French had sent a 90-gun warship, the *Charlemagne*, to Constantinople as a reminder of French naval strength. The Sultan submitted to French demands.

The French action in triggering the Holy Places dispute may be seen as a primary causal factor in the outbreak of war, although quite early into the conflict it ceased to have any real significance.

How did the Russians react?

The Russians were appalled at Turkey's response. Tsar Nicholas committed Russia to firm action in order to show that Russian influence over the Turks was greater than the French influence.

Britain and Austria were the only major European states with the power to be a threat and an interest in the affair. Nicholas was confident that he could rely on the Austrians not to challenge him. Austria was still recovering from internal revolt and was in a dire economic condition. In Britain, **Lord Aberdeen** had become head of a coalition government in December 1852. He feared and distrusted the French. The anti-Russian Palmerston had been removed as Foreign Secretary and replaced by **Lord John Russell**. Nicholas had already established a good working relationship with Aberdeen in 1844 when he had discussed plans for the partition of the Turkish Empire. Nicholas felt confident that he could rely on Britain not to frustrate Russian intentions in the Holy Places dispute.

The Menshikov Mission, 1853

The Russian Minister of Marine, Prince Menshikov, was sent to Constantinople to demand that the Sultan accept Russia's claim to protect all Christians living within the Turkish Empire. This was of supreme significance since about a third of the sultan's subjects were Christians. It amounted to Turkey submitting itself to Russian control. Russian diplomacy was based on bluster and menace and was characterised either by a remarkable disregard for international reaction or a complete inability to assess the attitudes of the great European powers.

To reinforce the demands, prior to Menshikov's mission, the Russians moved troops onto the borders of Moldavia and Wallachia. Despite Russian pressure of this kind, on 21 May 1853, Menshikov left Constantinople without a guarantee of Russia's rights to protect Christians in the empire. Diplomatic relations were broken off.

In July 1853, the Tsar ordered Russian troops to occupy the Turkish Black Sea principalities (**the Danubian Principalities**) of Moldavia and Wallachia. This military action was the main cause of the outbreak of war. Russia now had control of the mouth of the River Danube and had used force to occupy Turkish lands. Nicholas had simply confirmed what many Britons already knew; he was an aggressor and he did intend to take Constantinople and the vital route through the Straits.

How did the Turks react?

Turkey was not in a position to determine the course of events. The Sultan's strategy was either to make promises he did not intend to keep or to assume that Britain would ultimately come to Turkey's aid. This latter position was certainly the case after the British ambassador to Turkey, **Lord Stratford de Redcliffe**, encouraged the Sultan to make no concessions to Menshikov. The Turks were also influenced by the wave of Russophobia that the Menshikov Mission had created in Britain. This encouraged them to stand against the Russians. However, the idea that the Turks were merely puppets manipulated by the great powers is misleading. When the Sultan rejected Menshikov's demands, he knew that Britain would have to make a decision whether or not to support Turkey. Lord Aberdeen led a weak coalition government, faced with powerful anti-Russian opponents within its ranks and amongst the general public. The Sultan was fully aware of the power that he held and he used it to lure Britain into supporting Turkey.

It was significant that the Turks systematically rejected every opportunity to find a diplomatic solution to the crisis. This is particularly clear through their rejection of diplomatic initiatives taken by the Austrians in July 1853. They were determined to push Russia into a war in order to weaken Russia and thus reinforce their own security.

Lord Aberdeen finally submitted to the mounting pressure to take action. In July 1853, Britain sent a fleet to Besika Bay. Palmerston wanted it sent directly into the Black Sea in order to deliver a real warning of Britain's intentions to support the Turks militarily and to the point of war. The decision illustrates the divisions within Aberdeen's government. Aberdeen wanted peace but one that would ensure Constantinople's protection. Palmerston reflected the aggressive Russophobia of the day. His views were widely supported and his influence amongst the general public and other leading politicians was significant.

Lord Stratford de Redcliffe (1786-1880) A diplomat who served as British ambassador in Constantinople at various times between 1825 and 1851. He successfully influenced Turkish policy and encouraged some reforms within the Turkish Empire. He failed in his attempts to prevent the outbreak of the Crimean War.

The Vienna Note, July 1853

The Austrian Foreign Minister, **Count Buol**, organised a conference of ambassadors in Vienna largely because he feared Russia's control of the mouth of the Danube might pose a real threat to Austrian interests. Britain, France, Austria and Prussia attended the conference. The outcome was **the Vienna Note**.

Russia accepted the compromise but the Turks refused, partly because of the encouragement they received from de Redcliffe but largely because the sultan knew he could manipulate the British in order to strengthen his own position against the Russians. The evidence of this was clearly illustrated, when, in October 1853, Britain sent a fleet to Constantinople.

Turkey declared war on Russia in October 1853. This was yet another example of Turkey's confidence that Britain would support it and another example of Britain being drawn into providing support. The initiative undoubtedly lay with the Turks and not the British.

A cartoon entitled 'Bursting the Russian bubble' published in 1854 in the magazine Punch

Turkey entered the Black Sea with a fleet and the Russians destroyed it at Sinope with the loss of 4000 Turks. Russophobia was at its height in Britain and the Russian victory at Sinope generated an unprecedented level of anti-Russian feeling amongst the general public and the British press. The press referred to the 'massacre' of the Turks and emphasised the danger posed to both Britain and Turkey alike. Suddenly British interests were the same as those of Turkey in the face of a common enemy. Intervention on the side of Turkey was the only sensible course of action according to the press.

After the failure, in February 1854, of an Anglo–French demand that Russian troops leave the Principalities, Britain and France declared war on Russia on 28 March 1854.

THE CRIMEAN WAR, 1854–6

British and French war aims were significantly at variance. Napoleon III, Louis Napoleon's newly acquired title, wanted a quick victory in order to raise his prestige both domestically and internationally. Britain, certainly Palmerston, wanted a determined effort to destroy once and for all the Russian threat to Turkey. Austria was convinced that the war would endanger the stability of its empire, which was already in a fragile condition after the revolts of 1848. In the face of international opposition on this scale, Russia decided to withdraw from the Principalities in August 1854. As a result of this decision, there was, technically, no need for the war to continue since the occupation had been the primary cause of the war. In effect, the overt war aims of Britain and France had been achieved.

As the war was still continuing, it became necessary to establish the basis of a peace settlement. Austria proposed the Four Points.

- The Christians within the Turkish Empire were to be placed under European rather than Russian protection.
- The 1841 Straits Convention, which banned warships in the Black Sea, was to be revised in order to preserve the European balance of power.
- The Danube was to be a free river. No one state could control its use.
- Guarantees to protect the peoples of the Principalities were to be European rather than merely Russian.

Initially, the Tsar rejected the Four Points, but in November 1854, he accepted them. Once again the war should have ended but did not. Constantinople was secure and so too was the freedom of the Mediterranean from Russian influence. France had secured its honour and maintained its influence over Turkey. Clearly the war was being conducted to punish Russia and minimise the threat that may be posed to the Turkish Empire in the future. Britain's original war aims appeared to have changed, although for leaders like Palmerston, they had not.

Military action

Given the shift in their objectives, Britain and France were forced to carry out a naval expedition to attack Russia and that meant focusing on the Crimea. The Allied plan was that the French and British navies would isolate the Crimean peninsula while troops would seize **Sebastopol**.

The incompetence of the British military leaders meant that Sebastopol was not taken until September 1855. Poor leadership was shown on 25 October 1854 when the British launched a wasteful and largely futile attack against Russian artillery at Balaclava. **The Charge of the Light Brigade** was a classic example of British military blunders and one that enabled the Russians to remain in control of the only road between the British and the port where their supplies arrived into the Crimea.

In February 1855, Lord Aberdeen's government collapsed and Palmerston became Prime Minister. The French were reluctant to back the call for an aggressive war against the Russians. French honour had been satisfied and they were tired of war. A stalemate was reached in the Crimea. **Alexander II**, the new tsar, realising that neither side could make any meaningful military gains, agreed to talks and a peace conference was opened in Paris.

THE RESULTS OF THE CRIMEAN WAR

The Peace of Paris, 1856

Palmerston was determined to continue the war, but when peace came he wanted to ensure the most severe terms possible were imposed on the Russians. This had been his objective since the outbreak of war. For him, it was primarily a war to damage Russia and the protection of Turkey was a natural outcome of this objective.

The terms

- The Danubian Principalities were not to be protected solely by Russia. There was to be joint European protection.
- The existing rights and privileges of the Christians living within the empire were to be guaranteed by the Sultan.
- Turkey was to be admitted into the Concert of Europe and its **territorial integrity** guaranteed.
- There was to be freedom of navigation along the River Danube.
- Russia was to restore Southern Bessarabia to Turkey and this was to become part of Moldavia.

- The Straits Convention of 1841 was reaffirmed. This meant that both Russia and Turkey were forbidden from maintaining warships in the Black Sea.

What was the impact of the war and the Treaty of Paris on international relations?

The Crimean War ended the relationship that had existed between Russia and Austria since 1815. Austria had not supported the Russians. This marked the beginning of the collapse of the Concert of Europe. This was to become a crisis for Britain since the whole basis of British foreign policy in Europe was founded upon the preservation of the Concert. After 1856, Russia was prepared to allow Prussia to adopt a more aggressive role in central Europe at Austria's expense and that was to prove to be the death knell of the Concert of Europe.

After the war, Russia was determined to remove the restrictions imposed at Paris, particularly those linked to having naval access to the Black Sea. Ironically, the war had turned Palmerston's fears into actual Russian policy after 1856. In this sense, for Britain, the war was a resounding defeat. Britain's objectives of preserving a balance of power and restraining Russian expansionism by keeping the Turkish Empire intact were now under greater threat than at any previous point. The conclusion to the war had not addressed one of the war's causes – the Holy Places dispute.

Britain's military reputation had been damaged, the Concert of Europe was under immense strain, and Turkey remained a target of Russian expansionism. Britain had won the war but lost the peace.

SUMMARY QUESTIONS

1 Why was anti-Russian feeling so strong in Britain by 1854?

2 Explain why Britain went to war with Russia in 1854.

3 'The Crimean War was an unnecessary war.' Explain how far you agree with this view.

4 Explain the contribution of Russia and Turkey in the build up to war in 1854.

CHAPTER 3

The Balkans: what was Britain's involvement between 1875 and 1878?

By 1871, the Concert of Europe was no longer the framework within which European international relations operated. Britain's primary objective of protecting its interests through the preservation of a stable Europe based upon a balance of power had not changed, but Europe was no longer committed to the concept of international cooperation as the basis for preserving the balance of power and stability.

The turning point had come in 1871 when France lost the Franco–Prussian War.

- A new German Empire emerged in central Europe and with it a new element in European diplomacy.
- The French were determined to win allies in order to avoid the isolation they had faced during the war with Prussia. The new Germany was equally determined to keep France isolated and minimise the possible threat posed to its security by the prospect of French revenge.

THE DREIKAISERBUND, 1873

Germany confirmed its commitment to isolate France through this alliance. Russia, Austria–Hungary and Germany agreed on solidarity against social revolution. Although it was not a firm diplomatic or military alliance, the Dreikaiserbund was seen by Britain as a threat to the stability of Europe, and therefore to Britain. The question was would this alliance form the basis of Britain's isolation from influencing events in Europe and thereby protecting its interests? The issue of whether Britain would be able to preserve stability in Europe in the context of new **international alignments** was heightened still further when a crisis erupted in Turkish controlled South Eastern Europe (the Balkans).

> ### KEY TERM
>
> **International alignments**
> When states were allied to each other they were aligned. These alliances are not necessarily the result of formal treaty arrangements.

WHY DID BRITAIN GET INVOLVED IN THE BALKANS?

The Balkan problem

The Turkish Empire appeared to be disintegrating. In many parts of the Balkans, Turkish rule existed in name only. There was an increasing determination among the Christian peoples of the empire to gain national independence. Slav nationalism was growing rapidly and increasingly challenging the unity and stability of the Turkish Empire in Europe.

In general, there were three possible solutions to the problem.

- Implement internal reforms in order to reduce the demands for complete independence. This would be carried out by the Turks.
- The empire could be dismantled and shared out amongst the great powers.
- New independent states could be created by action undertaken by the great powers.

The attitudes of the powers of Europe

Russia

Russia posed as the long-term protector of the Christian peoples of the empire. Slav nationalism was supported by the Russians because it would weaken the Turkish Empire and thereby open up the opportunity for Russia to achieve its primary objective of controlling the Straits and Constantinople. These would give Russia access to the Mediterranean and '**warm water**'.

Austria–Hungary

Russian expansionism and Slav nationalism were a major concern to Austria. The fate of the Turkish Empire had significant economic, political and strategic consequences for Austria. Austria had access to the Mediterranean through the port of Trieste, but it was the River Danube that carried most of its trade. Russian control of the Straits and Constantinople would have placed a stranglehold on Austria's economic lifeline.

Furthermore, Austria's empire was a patchwork of different ethnic and national groups who might easily be encouraged to revolt if nationalism succeeded in the neighbouring Turkish Empire.

> **KEY TERM**
>
> **'Warm water'** Russia's northern coast was frozen for much of the year. Access to warm waters of the Mediterranean would have greatly enhanced Russia's position as a trading nation. It would also have significantly strengthened its naval power.

KEY EVENT

The new German Reich, 1871 Following Prussia's victory over the French in 1871, Germany was formally established as an independent new nation. Its first head of state was Kaiser Wilhelm I.

Austrian hopes of expansion to the north had been extinguished as a result of the formation of **the new German Reich** in 1871. In the south, the creation of Italy had had the same effect. Strategically, Austria's future lay in the east. The disintegration of the Turkish Empire was a viable option for the Austrians providing they received a slice of it.

Germany

Germany had no interest in the Balkans except in securing peace by whatever means was possible. Until there was an answer to the 'Eastern Question', each crisis would hold the possibility of Germany having to choose who to support, Russia or Austria. As the Dreikaiserbund amply illustrated, Germany wanted an alliance with both. The Balkans represented a source of division between Russia and Austria and a threat to Germany's plans for a new structure of European alliances.

France

France feared the weakening of Turkey. If newly independent states were created, France was convinced that they would be pro-Russian because they would perceive Russia as a protector and a natural religious and ethnic partner. Any extension of Russian influence in South Eastern Europe was seen by France as a threat to French interests in the Mediterranean and the Suez Canal zone. Equally, a stronger Russia as an ally to Germany would further weaken French influence in Europe, particularly if Austria, as the third Dreikaiserbund partner, was strengthened by the collapse of the Turkish Empire. The preservation of the Turkish Empire was central to French interests.

What were Disraeli's aims?

The problem that erupted in the Balkans was the first major international crisis facing Britain since the Crimean War. Disraeli's aims were clear:

- to prevent Russian territorial expansion into the Turkish Empire in Europe
- to prevent Russia gaining control of Constantinople and the Straits
- to preserve the territorial integrity of the Turkish Empire in Europe

- to disrupt the Dreikaiserbund and prevent any strengthening in the unity of its members.

The key issue here is why did Disraeli adopt these aims?

- For Britain, the Turkish Empire was the most effective barrier that could prevent Russia from expanding into South Eastern Europe and thereby possibly controlling Constantinople and the Straits. Such control would have given Russia unrestricted access to the Mediterranean. Disraeli regarded a Russian Mediterranean fleet as a primary threat to the security of the route to India through the Suez Canal. Protecting the route to India, and, indeed India itself, was symbolic of protecting the empire as a whole.

- The collapse of the Turkish Empire could lead to a general European war. The Dreikaiserbund had not united Russia, Germany and Austria to a point where they would readily share the empire out between themselves. War between the members was possible, particularly a war between Russia and Austria. The balance of power was at stake here and this was even more significant

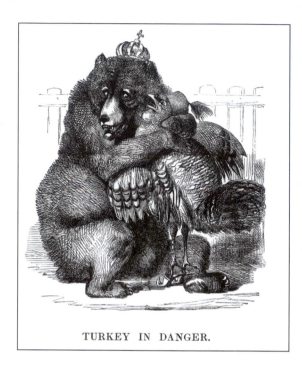

TURKEY IN DANGER.

A cartoon entitled 'Turkey in Danger' published in 1876 in the magazine Punch. The bear represents Russia and its attempts to gain control over Turkey.

given the collapse of the Concert of Europe. Disraeli maintained the fundamental British intention of preserving a balance of power as the foundation for the protection of British vital interests.

- The Dreikaiserbund was a potential threat to the balance of power in Europe. A three-power alliance, however fragile, represented a threat to stability, particularly at a time when the Turkish Empire was in such a volatile condition. Disraeli feared the rise of Germany, the state that had brought the Dreikaiserbund into being.

It was in the context of these conflicting aspirations of the European powers that events in the Turkish Empire unfolded.

HOW WAS BRITAIN INVOLVED IN THE BALKAN CRISIS, 1875–8?

In July 1875, the oppressed Serbs of Bosnia and Herzegovina rebelled against their Turkish rulers. Disraeli's immediate response was to support the first major diplomatic effort to end the fighting, **the Andrassy Note**.

The reasons for his actions were:

- Turkey agreed to accept the Note and its proposals
- it appeared to prevent the break-up of the Turkish empire, either into newly independent states or as parts of the empire being absorbed into Russia or Austria
- the Note was backed by the Dreikaiserbund, and Disraeli was anxious to ensure that the Dreikaiserbund did not seize the diplomatic initiative in the Balkans. Britain had to be directly involved if it was to influence the outcomes.

By early 1876, the revolts were still continuing. The Turks had simply refused to implement the Andrassy Note. This led, in May 1876, to a second diplomatic initiative in the form of **the Berlin Memorandum**.

Disraeli reversed his policy of support and immediately rejected the Memorandum because he was convinced that Britain must act outside any Dreikaiserbund initiatives. He was certain that its members were secretly planning to dismember the Turkish Empire in Europe.

To underline Britain's independent policy, Disraeli sent a fleet to Besika Bay. The Turks saw this as British support for them while the Dreikaiserbund saw it as a clumsy piece of Palmerstonian style aggression. Turkey simply rejected the Memorandum.

Disraeli's actions had merely delayed international intervention and further deepened the growing crisis in the Balkans. He appeared to be more interested in challenging the Dreikaiserbund than in promoting a diplomatic solution in the Balkans.

By the summer of 1876, the revolts had spread into Bulgaria, Serbia and Montenegro. The Turkish response was to massacre thousands of Bulgarians. Disraeli's pro-Turkish position created a new problem. There was a profound anti-Turkish reaction throughout British public

KEY EVENT

The Andrassy Note, December 1875 The Austro–Hungarian Foreign Minister, Count Andrassy, sent a diplomatic message to the Turks proposing religious and economic reforms, which might restore peace in Bosnia and Herzegovina.

KEY EVENT

The Berlin Memorandum, May 1876 This attempted to broker a ceasefire in Bosnia and Herzegovina and implement the proposals in the Andrassy Note. It was the work of the Dreikaiserbund.

opinion in response to the Turkish atrocities against the Bulgarians. Disraeli's greatest political rival, Gladstone, was a prime mover in stimulating this. How could Disraeli adopt a hard-line anti-Russian stance as Russia threatened the Turks in defence of the Bulgarians and the Christian peoples of the Turkish Empire? His policy had been seriously undermined.

The Conference of Constantinople, 1876–7

Disraeli was quick to seize the initiative by proposing a European great power conference to be held at Constantinople. There was a degree of cooperation and agreement was reached that Bosnia and Herzegovina should unite under nominal Turkish rule. It was also agreed that Serbia and Montenegro should increase territorially from Turkish controlled land and that Bulgaria should be granted self-governing status.

The whole process came to a stop when the Sultan of Turkey simply refused to accept the agreements. Turkey's military victories against the Serbs and Montenegrins had convinced him that compromise was not necessary. As far as the Russians were concerned, there was only one possible course of action in response to Turkey's refusal.

The Russo–Turkish War, 1877

In April 1877, the Russians declared war on Turkey. Disraeli's position had to be one of neutrality given the events surrounding the Bulgarian massacres. Russia assured Britain that the security of Egypt, the Suez Canal and the freedom of Constantinople would be guaranteed. Despite this, British neutrality proved to be only temporary. The Russians overran the Turks and, by January 1878, threatened Constantinople. A British fleet was despatched to protect Constantinople and force Russia into a ceasefire.

Although public opinion was clamouring for war against Russia, Disraeli's policy was based on threats rather than direct action. War was the last thing Disraeli wanted because he had no committed allies to unite with against the Russians. However, Disraeli was also convinced that the most effective way to deter the Russians was to make them believe that Britain would be prepared to go to war if its interests in the Eastern Mediterranean were seriously threatened. Diplomacy was not enough, hence the use of

British naval power as a show of strength and ultimate intent. Disraeli was willing to undertake this action without the immediate support of other European powers. He was determined to prevent the Russians from breaking the terms of the Peace of Paris, 1856. The action was enough to pressurise the Russians into forcing the Turks to agree to peace talks.

The Treaty of San Stephano, 1878

The Balkans after the Treaty of San Stephano, 1878

Under the terms of this treaty:

- Serbia, Montenegro and Romania were to become independent states and slightly expanded in size
- Bulgaria was to be greatly increased in size and given access to the Ægean Sea. It was also to become a self-governing principality under Russian protection
- Dobrujia was to go to Romania
- Russia was to recover Southern Bessarabia.

Significantly, the Treaty made no direct reference to Constantinople or to the control of the Straits. To that extent, British interests were not threatened. However, Russian influence in a greatly enlarged Bulgaria had major implications for Britain. The Treaty had effectively removed any significant presence of the Turkish Empire in Europe and replaced it with a significantly increased Russian presence. Strategically, the Straits and Constantinople were more vulnerable than they had been at any previous point.

The impact of this situation was that the balance of power in Europe had been seriously compromised as Russian influence in South Eastern Europe expanded. The Straits were under threat and therefore the possibility of a Russian Mediterranean fleet was made ever more real. Finally, the long-term security of the remaining part of the Turkish Empire in Europe was in grave doubt. All these factors heightened British concern. The very foundations of British foreign policy in Europe, and indeed British imperial policy and the protection of imperial trade, were being challenged.

Austria, along with Britain, demanded a second international conference. Disraeli backed up this demand by sending 7000 Indian troops to Malta. Germany offered Berlin as a neutral venue for a second conference.

The Congress of Berlin, 1878

Disraeli dominated the proceedings at the Congress. He ensured success from the British perspective through a series of pre-congress meetings. Russia agreed to withdraw its support for a greatly increased Bulgaria, and Turkey agreed to sell the Mediterranean island of Cyprus to Britain in return for a formal guarantee to defend Turkey from Russian aggression. The main points agreed were:

- Big Bulgaria was to be dismembered and three new regions established: an independent, smaller Bulgaria was to be created in the north, Eastern Rumelia was to become a partly self-governing province of the Turkish Empire with a Christian governor, and Macedonia was to be fully restored under Turkish rule.
- Serbia, Montenegro and Romania were to become independent states.

- Austria was given the right to occupy, but not to annex, Bosnia and Herzegovina.
- The Turks agreed to introduce religious reforms.
- For the rest, the terms of the San Stephano Treaty remained intact.

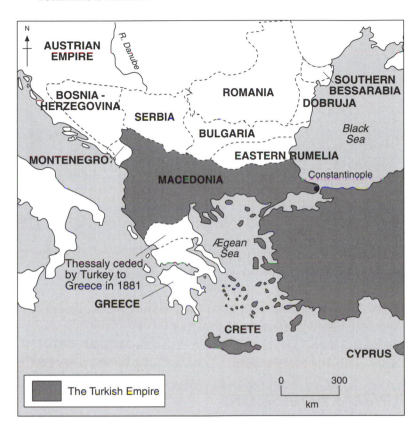

The Balkans after the Congress of Berlin, 1878

HOW SIGNIFICANT WERE THE RESULTS OF DISRAELI'S POLICIES IN THE BALKANS?

The highpoint of Disraeli's policies in the Balkans came with the Congress of Berlin and it is through an assessment of the position after the Congress that Disraeli's achievements may be measured.

- The 'Eastern Question' was not resolved. The primary issue of long-lasting peace and the security of the Turkish Empire had not been achieved. The empire had not been offered cast-iron guarantees of protection from the great powers and territorially it had been weakened a reduction in its size. Despite this, Disraeli had succeeded in preserving some territory for the Turks and this was enough to enable them to remain some form of barrier to Russian expansionism.

- Disraeli had not removed the prospect of regional instability in Eastern Europe. Serbia and Montenegro were suspicious of Austrian influence in the region and the Bulgarians resented their territorial losses.
- There were some significant achievements as a result of Disraeli's policies. He had gained the strategically important island of Cyprus. This was a vital advantage, particularly in view of Britain's growing commitment to Egypt and the Suez Canal route to India.
- By restraining Russian expansionism, Disraeli had contributed to the preservation of the balance of power in Europe.

Overall, the primary objectives of British foreign policy had been fulfilled using Disraeli's policies and this had been done using the threat of war rather than the reality of it.

PUNCH, OR THE LONDON CHARIVARI.—JULY 20, 1878.

"HUMPTY-DUMPTY"!

"HUMPTY-DUMPTY SAT ON A WALL;
HUMPTY-DUMPTY HAD A GREAT FALL:
DIZZY, WITH CYPRUS, AND ALL THE QUEEN'S MEN,
HOPES TO SET HUMPTY-DUMPTY UP AGAIN."

A cartoon entitled 'Humpty-Dumpty!' published in 1878 in the magazine Punch

SUMMARY QUESTIONS

1 How successful were Disraeli's policies in the Balkans, 1875–8, in protecting British interests?

2 Explain two reasons why Disraeli's policies in the Balkans between 1875 and 1878 might be regarded as a success in terms of protecting British interests.

3 Explain why keeping the Turkish Empire intact was so important to Britain between 1875 and 1878.

4 Explain the ways in which Russian policy in the Balkans influenced what Britain did there between 1875 and 1878.

CHAPTER 4

Why did Britain want to expand its imperial influence in Africa between 1868 and 1902?

THE POSITION BEFORE 1880

Britain and Africa

Britain's possessions in Africa before 1880 were very few. The largest area of British control was in South Africa. Cape Colony was a formal British colony and Natal, on the Cape's north-eastern border, had been added in 1843. This had been done to strengthen Britain's influence in the Indian Ocean. This was useful in terms of protecting the routes to India and Australia. Britain also claimed the right to control the foreign affairs of the Boer republics of the Orange Free State and the Transvaal. In West Africa, Britain controlled a few small coastal areas consisting of Gambia, Sierra Leone, the Gold Coast and Lagos, which were formally annexed in 1861. In North and East Africa, Britain had no colonies. In the east, a trade agreement with the Sultan of Zanzibar was the extent of any British presence. The interior of Africa remained untouched by any British influence. By 1872, Cape Colony had been granted self-governing dominion status. Britain's other colonies in West Africa remained as **dependent colonies**.

Britain and imperialism

Before the last quarter of the nineteenth century, Britain had no structured or official policy based upon imperial expansion. Essentially, Britain's approach to empire was founded upon two concepts: informal imperialism and formal imperialism.

Informal imperialism

The advantage of informal imperialism was that Britain did not need to establish territorial control. There were no direct costs to Britain in terms of establishing control over territory and maintaining that control. The primary purpose of an informal empire was to establish a purely economic influence. Britain could access profitable markets

---

> **KEY TERM**
>
> **Dependent colonies**
> Colonies that were not primarily settlement colonies for British people such as Canada. Dependent colonies existed as trading or naval bases and had few British settlers. Such colonies were generally ruled directly from Britain, although India was an exception to this arrangement.

for British manufactured goods and obtain cheap raw materials. There was no intention to rule. The process was one of economic exploitation at minimum cost. In Africa, for example, although Britain had a small territorial colonial presence, there was an extensive network of relationships with local tribal leaders established for purely economic opportunities.

Free trade was an important aspect of this form of imperialism. By the 1860s, free trade had been achieved and Britain was able to negotiate free trade agreements. This meant that informal imperialism could flourish. There was no need for Britain to conqueror territory in order to exploit economic opportunities when free trade offered even greater opportunities at no cost.

Informal imperialism enabled Britain to exercise global commercial influence. The triumph of free trade reinforced and strengthened the commitment to an informal empire because it brought to an end the monopoly British traders had over Britain's colonial markets.

Formal imperialism
Beyond the informal empire that Britain had developed, there also existed an empire based on territorial control. Those colonies that were regarded as settlements for Britons were awarded dominion status. This gave them extensive freedom for self-government while Britain retained control of their foreign policies and their defence. Dependent status was afforded to the rest.

Although the protection of the formal empire played a significant role in British foreign policy decisions before 1880, there was no determination to expand the formal empire. Economic interests were all-important to Britain. When free trade was finally achieved, it was the dependent colonies that suffered most. India, for example, was unable to introduce measures to protect its own economy. This enabled British traders to flood India with British imports. Britain's economic interests were flourishing and there was certainly no intention, before 1880, to promote further conquests in Africa.

The key question becomes why did this attitude change? After 1889, there was a massive expansion of Britain's formal empire in Africa.

WHAT WAS BRITAIN'S ROLE IN THE PARTITION OF AFRICA?

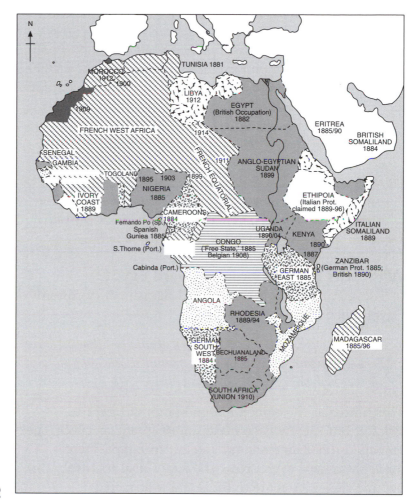

Colonial Africa, 1912

Between approximately 1880 and 1900, about 90 per cent of the continent was seized by Britain, France, Germany and Belgium. Other European states such as Portugal and Spain already had a foothold in Africa. Britain acquired the lion's share by taking about 5 million square miles of territory. France got about 3.5 million square miles, while Germany, Belgium and Italy shared a further 2.5 million square miles. The powers of Europe were greedy for African lands but for Britain this was a significant shift in policy. Gladstone, although not openly anti-imperialist, favoured a policy of colonial self-defence.

The scale and pace of Britain's expansionism may be understood through a simple timeline.

HEINEMANN ADVANCED HISTORY

1882	The occupation of Egypt.
1884–5	Somaliland in East Africa and Bechuanaland in the south are declared British protectorates.
1886	A Royal Charter was granted to **the Niger Company** which predated the creation of two Nigerian protectorates in West Africa by 1899.
1889	Cecil Rhodes' **British South Africa Company** was granted a charter to extend British control northwards from Bechuanaland into what was ultimately to become Northern and Southern Rhodesia.
1894–5	Uganda was declared a British possession and Britain took over direct control of Kenya from **the Imperial British East Africa Company**.
1898	The Sudan was brought into the empire.

What was Britain's policy toward Egypt?

In 1860, Palmerston had identified British policy towards Egypt when he said:

> *What we wish about Egypt is that it should be attached to the Turkish Empire, which is security against it belonging to another European power. We wish to trade with Egypt.*

This hinted at the economic importance of Egypt to Britain, but there was no expansionist intent in 1860. The French also had an economic interest in Egypt. French money was used to construct the Suez Canal in 1869. This became the quick route to India and it attracted considerable British investment in Egypt and in the canal itself. Furthermore, Egypt produced high quality cotton, which was much sought after by British textile manufacturers.

In response to nationalist riots led by **Colonel Arabi** in June 1882, Britain invaded Egypt and by October the revolts were crushed. Although Egypt was part of the Turkish Empire, its ruler, the Khedive, Tewfik, was left merely as a figurehead. The government of Egypt devolved into British hands. The reasons for this action, particularly in view of Gladstone's reluctance to expand the British Empire, may be explained as follows.

- Economic – Britain had significant financial investments in Egypt and these needed to be protected; trade with Egypt was vital for the British economy.
- Imperial – The Suez Canal was the route to India. It represented a vital trade route and was of supreme importance strategically. Britain had to control the canal as a means of protecting India and all the economic advantages for Britain that India offered.
- Political – Egyptian nationalism would have freed Egypt from the control of Turkey and enabled Egypt to form alliances with European states. Britain's greatest fear was that French influence in Egypt would increase. This could have threatened not only Britain's economic interests in Egypt but also the route to India.

This initial act of imperial expansionism in Africa was the outcome not of a planned policy to exploit the opportunity to intervene, but of simple economic priorities. Stability in the Eastern Mediterranean was essential for British economic interests and that priority had not changed through this occupation.

However, the occupation may be regarded as a turning point in European attitudes towards Africa. It was after this occupation that the scramble for African lands by European powers began in earnest.

How did British influence in West Africa develop?

Britain already had a colonial presence in West Africa by 1880 in the shape of Gambia, Sierra Leone and the Gold Coast, and a foothold in Nigeria at Lagos, acquired in 1861. The attraction of Nigeria lay in the palm oil trade. Palm oil was used as an industrial lubricant and as the base for making soap and candles. This economic enterprise was based not on formal colonial control but through the trade networks characteristic of the 'informal empire'. It was dominated by the Royal Niger Company.

This informal arrangement was threatened when other European states, France, Germany and Belgium, began to show expansionist interests in the region. The base of French expansionism was their existing colony at Senegal from where they wanted to develop a West African Empire dominating the inland trade. The danger was that the important trade along the river Niger would be under threat from this French expansionism.

Similar region pressure came in 1885 when the Belgians set up **the Congo Free State** in order to exploit the thriving rubber trade there. Not only were British economic interests beginning to be threatened, but there was also the issue of international rivalry. If other European powers began to establish extensive territorial control in West Africa, Britain could not simply ignore this and maintain its informal empire strategy. In 1884, the situation was further complicated when Germany seized Togoland and the Cameroons.

In 1885, a conference in Berlin agreed that there should be free trade in the Congo basin and recognised British interests along the River Niger. Significantly, there was also agreement reached about the process of annexation of territory in West Africa in the future. Out of this agreement emerged the British colony of Nigeria.

The motivating force in British West African colonisation lay typically in economic interests but, perhaps more importantly, in Britain's determination not to allow other European states to grab land that might threaten this trade. The West African experience set the ground rules for imperialism in the region.

What were British interests in East Africa?

KEY PLACE

The Congo Free State, 1885–1908 This was a private kingdom owned by King Leopold II of Belgium. It included the entire area now known as Zaire. In 1908, it became part of Belgium's formal empire and was known from then on as the Belgian Congo.

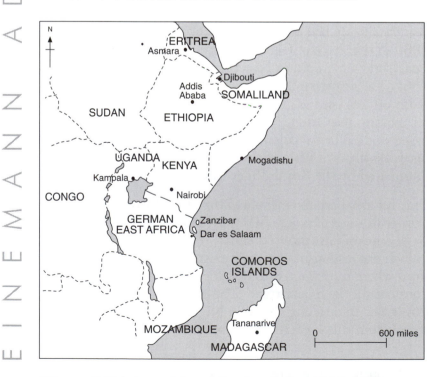

East Africa, c.1895

In East Africa, as in the north in Egypt, there were vital British interests at stake. The island of Zanzibar imported significant quantities of manufactured goods from Britain and India, and its total import and export trade was measured at about £2 million. It was a major trading point for the East African interior from which came ivory and leather goods and into which went textiles from Manchester, brass from Birmingham and Sheffield steel.

Britain's primary interest was trade and East Africa had huge economic potential for future development but this did not equate to formal colonisation. The critical factor came when German and French explorers became interested in the area. This raised the prospect of a major threat to British trade and the creation of a French or German naval base on the coast, which might threaten the routes to India and the Far East. However, it was Germany who seized the initiative when **Otto von Bismarck** announced the creation of a German protectorate in East Africa.

A diplomatic agreement was reached in 1886 to divide East Africa into British and German spheres of interest, but the agreement appeared to offer greater economic opportunities to the Germans than to the British. In early 1888, Sir William MacKinnon launched the Imperial British East Africa Company, backed by investors such as the Manchester cotton manufacturer James Hutton, the brewer Henry Younger and the shipping magnate George Mackenzie. It was pressure from MacKinnon's company that finally established a British presence of any scale in East Africa. The British expanded into Uganda, Kenya, Zanzibar and Somaliland.

The key factors in British colonialism in East Africa were:

- the economic importance of the area and the pressure put on the government to protect and expand the economic opportunities
- a determination to resist any imbalance in the land grabbing. If Germany expanded its influence in the area, then so must Britain. It was, however, significant that Lord Salisbury was reluctant to establish formal British control and preferred the diplomatic approach.

KEY PERSON

Otto von Bismarck (1815-98) In 1847 he became a member of the Prussian parliament and then the Prime Minister of Prussia between 1862 and 1890. He was the first Chancellor of the newly created German Empire in 1871, a post he held until 1890. His main priority was to strengthen Germany, particularly through alliances with Russia and Austria.

There was also a strong feeling in government at this time that it was not the role of government to provide capital investment in any economic enterprises. That was the role of entrepreneurs. Again, this underlined the reluctance of British political leaders to commit to a formal occupation of territory until the initial stages had been backed by economic aid from private groups.

WHO WAS TO CONTROL SOUTHERN AFRICA: BRITISH OR BOERS?

The development of British imperialism in Southern Africa was intimately bound up with the **Boer settlers** in the Transvaal and the Orange Free State. Relations between the British and the Boers had never been good, but, in 1877, the Boers turned to Britain for help against an uprising by the Zulu tribes in the Transvaal. Britain was willing to help because this was seen as an opportunity to consolidate British rule in Southern Africa. The British defeated the Zulus and annexed the Transvaal.

WHY DID THE FIRST BOER WAR BREAK OUT IN 1881?

In an attempt to restore their independence, the Boers successfully attacked British forces at Majuba Hill in 1881. Gladstone, reluctant to be involved in a colonial war, agreed to the Pretoria Convention. Britain's determination to control Southern Africa was reflected in the fact that at the Convention the Transvaal was forced to accept British **suzerainty**. In the face of continued Boer objections, the suzerainty was withdrawn through the **Treaty of London** in 1884. In effect, the Transvaal was left to control its own affairs except in matters of foreign policy. This was a vital form of control for Britain because it placed important constraints on the Transvaal's ability to form links with Britain's European rivals, particularly Germany. The situation was to be transformed from 1886 when gold was discovered in the Transvaal. The Boers were farmers not miners, but they wanted to exploit this new-found wealth. Miners and traders flooded into the Transvaal from abroad. The Boers called them '**uitlanders**' or outsiders. This opened up opportunities for one of the most influential figures in British colonial expansion in Africa from the 1880s, Cecil Rhodes.

KEY PEOPLE

Boer settlers These were the descendents of the first Dutch settlers on the Cape. In order to escape British control and preserve the independence of their culture and church, they had embarked on a 'trek' northwards where they established two new settlements of Transvaal and the Orange Free State. These were recognised as independent Boer republics in 1854.

KEY TERM

Suzerainty The right of a state to hold nominal control over the affairs of another state. The Transvaal did not have complete independence from British control under this agreement.

KEY TREATY

The Treaty of London, 1884 This treaty effectively recognised the independence of the Transvaal.

KEY PEOPLE

Uitlanders This was the term used by the Boers in the Transvaal and the Orange Free State to describe new immigrants in the 19th century who came to exploit the gold and diamond riches in the region.

Cecil Rhodes (1853–1902)
Rhodes went to Africa at the age of seventeen and became a millionaire through diamond and gold mining enterprises. By the mid-1880s, he was committed to the idea of creating a great British Empire in Africa. In 1889, he founded the British South Africa Company and used this trading organisation to push British control northwards from Cape Colony. In 1890, he established Southern Rhodesia, a territory named after himself. This was pushed further north the following year. Rhodes' personal dream was to establish a railway under British control and running through British colonies, from Cairo to the Cape. He was a ruthless imperialist whose actions frequently caused major problems for the British government and contributed significantly to the outbreak of the Second Anglo–Boer War in 1899.

The Matabele War, 1893-94 Jameson led a raid against Matabeleland. About 50 whites were killed in the conflict. The war lasted only 3 months and resulted in a victory for Jameson by January 1894. The outcome strengthened colonial imperialism in southern Africa.

WHAT PART DID CECIL RHODES PLAY?

Although British governments did not always share **Cecil Rhodes**' commitment to a continent wide empire in Africa, they did see him as a vital component in protecting Britain's influence in Southern Africa.

By 1884, it was becoming increasingly clear that Boer settlers were penetrating onto Bechuanaland. There was the possibility that the Boers might link up with German colonists who were settling in what was to become German South West Africa. This could have led to the isolation of British controlled Southern Africa from the supposedly mineral rich Zambesia to the north. The possibility of a German–Transvaal alliance was of great concern to Britain at this time. Rhodes not only saw the opportunity for colonial expansion but also for the expansion of his own personal wealth if he could access the economic potential in the Zambesia region. Bechuanaland was crucial in this process. In December 1884, Britain declared Bechuanaland a British protectorate.

In 1881, Rhodes had become a member of the Cape parliament and he had commented: 'Africa is still lying ready for us. It is our duty to take it.' In 1889, he secured a charter for his British South Africa Company (BSAC). Rhodes knew that he could exploit the government's attitude of empire by using his company to administer and control new territories on behalf of the British government. Rhodes' position was strengthened still further when he became Prime Minister of Cape Colony in 1890. The BSAC functioned, in practice, like an independent colonising organisation. It had received rights for farming and mining in Mashonaland. Attempts by the native population to challenge the company resulted in **the Matabele War** of 1893–4.

Not only was Rhodes motivated by economic greed and a sense of imperial destiny, but also a profoundly racist approach towards Africans. At the age of 23, Rhodes had written:

Why should we not form a secret society with but one object, the furtherance of the British Empire and the bringing of the whole uncivilised world under British rule, for making the Anglo–Saxon race but one empire.

There was considerable support for these views in Britain and within the government.

By 1895, Rhodes' company had eliminated all effective opposition to his control of Rhodesia and Nyasaland. The only barrier to his dream of British supremacy in Southern Africa was the Transvaal. The Boers were interested in the creation of a federation of South African states, of which the Transvaal would become a leading power. There was a fear in Britain that such a union might be too weak to resist German influence in the region. For Britain, a major strategic issue was emerging. Britain needed a reason to attack the Transvaal. Ostensibly, this was the treatment of British nationals working in the Transvaal who were regarded as second-class citizens. The Colonial Secretary, Joseph Chamberlain, gave his secret blessing to what was to become a disastrous raid against the Transvaal.

THE JAMESON RAID, 1895

With the support of Cecil Rhodes, the chief administrator of the BSAC, **Dr Starr Jameson** and about 500 troops launched an attack on the Transvaal hoping to generate an armed uprising amongst the uitlanders against the Boers. The raid was a disaster: there was no uprising. Rhodes resigned as Cape Prime Minister and the Boers were convinced of Britain's involvement in the affair. The raid put the Transvaal and Britain on a collision course because one of them now had to establish its superiority in South Africa. As one South African commented: 'The ambition of the Transvaal to become the rising power in the land is beyond doubt and I don't think we shall all quiet down again until the question is settled one way or another.' The issue finally came to a head in 1899.

THE SECOND BOER WAR, 1899–1902

The issue was who was to control South Africa, the British or the Boers? Although the Transvaal had huge economic resources in the form of diamonds and gold, the primary concern for Britain was one of strategic importance. The Cape had to be free from Boer threats and the Boer links to Germany. The Cape was a vital strategic factor in Britain's security because it controlled a route to India.

Chamberlain certainly regarded the freedom of the Boers to control their own domestic affairs as weakening Britain's power. For Chamberlain Britain must have complete control in order to protect its interests. Chamberlain was fundamentally in favour of expanding Britain's empire. Stability in Europe had ended and it was up to Britain to promote its own power through imperial expansionism. Consolidating British control of Southern Africa was part of Chamberlain's strategy to achieve this vision.

The governor of Cape Colony, **Alfred Milner**, negotiated with the Boers but, in October 1899, war broke out and lasted until May 1902. The war ended with the Peace of Vereeniging. The Boer republics of the Transvaal and the Orange Free State were annexed and their peoples became part of the British Empire. In 1907, the two former republics became self-governing colonies.

SUMMARY QUESTIONS

1   Why did Britain take part in the 'scramble for Africa'?

2   How far did Britain's approach to imperialism change after about 1880?

3   Assess the importance of economic factors influencing Britain's attitude towards imperial expansion in Africa after 1880.

4   How important were the Boers as a factor in British interests in Southern Africa after 1880?

CHAPTER 5

Why did so many Britons support imperialism between 1880 and 1902?

From about 1880, Britain adopted a more aggressive form of imperialism and there was extensive support for this amongst the British people. Support was particularly strong within the Conservative Party and amongst the middle classes. Commitment to imperialism amongst the working classes was less clearly defined but certainly present. The working class were less easily convinced of the benefits, for them, of patriotism. The empire may have provided some employment but it did not lead to high pay and rising prosperity. The key issue is what factors helped to shape this enthusiasm for imperialism and how effective were these in reinforcing the commitment to imperialism amongst the British people?

Economic issues were particularly significant. All social classes in Britain were able to recognise the advantages an empire offered to each of them. The working class gained employment and some prosperity, as did the middle class. The rich, the investor class and the industrialists benefited from the massive economic opportunities the empire presented. What had developed after 1880 was a new conception of imperialism amongst politicians and the key figure in the process was Joseph Chamberlain.

WHAT WAS THE IMPACT OF JOSEPH CHAMBERLAIN?

From 1895, Chamberlain promoted his message as loudly and as widely as he could. As Colonial Secretary in Salisbury's administration, he was in a good position to do this.

Economic opportunities

The last quarter of the nineteenth century saw a decline in Britain's economic dominance that led to falling profits and rising unemployment. The empire offered a lifeline to offset this economic decline. The protective tariffs imposed on British goods by competitors, such as the USA and Germany, served only to make Britain's economic future even less certain. Closer direct control of colonial territory would remove the uncertainty of foreign competition and guarantee Britain ready markets. Under Chamberlain, economic priorities demanded that Britain's imperial power expand through direct control rather than depend upon the loose trading arrangements currently operating.

Social reform

The profits generated through imperial control would benefit investors and workers as well as helping to finance the radical social reforms Chamberlain wanted. The elimination of poverty and the revitalisation of urban industrial areas were fundamental to Chamberlain's thinking.

'Civilising the heathens'

For Chamberlain, Britain had a moral responsibility to bring civilisation and Christianity to the native peoples. Chamberlain's influence on popular attitudes towards imperialism was significant. Many elements of his vision of a great global empire with Britain at the centre were taken up through the media and popular entertainment. Central to his thinking was the notion that Britain was helping the uncivilised and racially inferior native peoples. This image appealed to the majority of people in Britain.

His ideas of economic security through direct imperial control appealed on a more practical level. The outcome of his contribution to the popularisation of imperialism was the vision of Britain as a dominant world power, and dominance was always going to win popular support.

THE MEDIA AND PROPAGANDA: WHAT PART DID THEY PLAY?

Propaganda is the art of convincing someone to believe something by using ideas and images that are persuasive and believable. Pro-imperialist propaganda was widespread after 1880. For propaganda to be effective, the message and the images needed to:

- be simple and easily accessible to most people
- be repeated frequently
- be believable and therefore not a complete lie or an excessive exaggeration
- be based on something the audience may already have believed, however slight
- maintain the interest of the audience.

The media was a superb vehicle for imperialist propaganda because it could reach the masses at every age level. There may not have been a coordinated or deliberate plan to indoctrinate, but the financial incentives to exploit imperialism as a popular theme to sell publications certainly made a massive contribution towards shaping popular attitudes on imperialism.

Children's literature

Children were a target of much imperialist literature. Some examples of imperialist literature aimed at children were *The Boys' Own Paper*, *Magnet*, *Gem*, *Wizard* and *Union Jack*. All the boys' magazines included heroic figures who defended their bit of the empire. A publisher of many of these papers stated:

> *These boys' journals aimed from the first at the encouragement of physical strength and patriotism, of international travel and exploration, and pride in our empire. It has been said that boys' papers did more to provide recruits for our navy and army...than anything else.*

The question arises as to why boys were the target and why these themes of heroic patriotism and commitment to the empire were emphasised. The stories were designed to appeal to a boy's 'natural' interest in physical strength, adventure and exploration. It was relatively easy for the storywriters to place these into the context of the British Empire and then introduce the ideas of patriotism and duty. The attitudes of the 1890s towards gender roles were fairly well drawn. Males were the protectors and the 'active' sex, while females were the basis of domestic family life. Magazines and books for girls encouraged them to accept the role of wife or mother to the men who were building and protecting the empire.

Boys' journals encouraging physical strength and patriotism

The emphasis on imperialism was used because it was seen as the most effective way to sell the magazines. There was no coordinated plan, of which publishers were a part, to use boys' magazines to promote pro-imperialistic propaganda designed to indoctrinate the young. The magazines reflected, and to some extent shaped, the mood of the time driven by a desire for commercial profit.

In addition to the magazines, numerous novels were also written for children based on imperial themes. One of the

KEY PEOPLE

G. A. Henty (1832–1902)

He had been a war correspondent in Africa and had first-hand experience of the nature of Britain's colonial presence. 25 of his novels focused on poor but decent orphan boys who met real 'heroes' of the empire, such as General Kitchener and Clive of India. Henty published titles such as *With Clive in India*, *The Dash for Khartoum* and *By Sheer Pluck: A Tale of the Ashanti*.

Rudyard Kipling (1865–1936)

Kipling was born in Bombay, India, the son of a schoolmaster. He was educated in England and in 1882 he returned to India as a newspaper reporter on the *Civil and Military Gazette*. He soon became noted for his verse and short stories, which both focused on imperial, patriotic and military issues. He played a leading role in helping to shape the attitudes and values of the British public on imperialism. In 1907, Kipling was awarded the Nobel Prize for Literature. Perhaps the most significant indicator of his views is expressed in his work *Kim*, a masterpiece of imperialism which emphasised Britain's right to rule India. He campaigned for a strong government approach to preserving the empire. The outbreak of the First World War convinced him that the empire was doomed and he became increasingly disillusioned about Britain's place in the world.

best-known writers was **G. A. Henty**. The very wide audience his books and magazines reached and their undoubted popularity with that audience meant that they inadvertently succeeded in reinforcing a sense of national pride and national identity and therefore did indoctrinate young minds.

Popular literature

One of the greatest contributors to imperialist propaganda for adult consumption was **Rudyard Kipling**. He was a consummate propagandist whose work revealed a deliberate intent to manipulate British public opinion. Like all good propagandists, Kipling exploited the ideas and beliefs he knew already existed in embryonic form in the minds of his readers. He was convinced that the great majority of the British people held racist views and believed in their own superiority as a race. Kipling's work presented Britons as having a duty to help the less fortunate and inferior peoples of the empire. Patronising though his work was, it reinforced and strengthened British racism and the idea that those who lived within the empire were fortunate that Britain was willing to help them. Britons were to be proud of the burden they shouldered on behalf of others as expressed in his poem, *The White Man's Burden*:

> *Take up the white man's burden –*
> *Send forth the best ye breed –*
> *Go bind your sons to exile*
> *To serve your captive's need;*
> *To wait in heavy harness*
> *On fluttered folk and wild –*
> *Your new-caught, sullen peoples*
> *Half-devil and half-child.*

Kipling's verse also had strong links with religion and this was another way to reinforce imperialism, particularly amongst the churchgoing middle class. A classic example of this comes in his poem *Recessional*:

> *God of our fathers, known of old,*
> *Lord of our far-flung battle-line,*
> *Beneath whose awful hand we hold*
> *Dominion over palm and pine –*
> *Lord of Hosts, be with us yet,*
> *Lest we forget – lest we forget!*

Why did so many Britons support imperialism between 1880 and 1902?   59

The popular press

Much of the newspaper industry by the late nineteenth century was in the hands of pro-imperialist owners. Lord Harmsworth, who founded the *Daily Mail*, was a classic example of this. As with children's publications, the popular press magnates knew that stories that glamourised the empire and offered accounts of colonial conflicts that produced heroes would make popular reading amongst the British general public.

In September 1898, British forces faced 50,000 Sudanese troops at Omdurman. **Winston Churchill**, a young reporter with the cavalry, wrote an article for the *Morning Post* newspaper. In it he commented:

Highland troops at the Battle of Atbara, April 1898

We thought them spearmen, for we were within 300 yards and they had fired no shot. Suddenly, as the regiment began to trot, they opened a heavy, severe and dangerous fire. The trumpets sounded 'right-wheel into line' and on the instant the regiment began to gallop in excellent order towards the riflemen.

The article presents the British action as a glorious episode in military history. The reality of this engagement was that during the charge that Churchill witnessed, 300 British cavalry charged against what they thought were 150 Sudanese. Behind these were a further 3000 unseen Sudanese. The charge continued and within two minutes 70 cavalrymen and 119 horses were killed or wounded. The press presented this military blunder as a feat of remarkable courage and a glorious action for the British. During the Battle of Omdurman, 11,000 Sudanese soldiers were killed at the hands of the British and this was exactly what made newspapers sell.

KEY PERSON

Winston Churchill (1874-1965) Initially a soldier and reporter, Churchill became a Liberal Party MP in 1900. He remained a Liberal until 1923. He was First Lord of the Admiralty (1911-15) and Chancellor of the Exchequer (1924-29). In 1940 he returned to high office, after a period in the political wilderness, as Prime Minister leading a wartime coalition government. He was defeated in the 1945 election, but returned as Prime Minister between 1951 and 1955.

By the late nineteenth century, about 90 per cent of the population of Britain was literate and therefore able to read newspapers. New printing technology made the papers cheap to produce and allowed for mass circulation. This was a perfect formula for using the press as an agent for mass propaganda supporting imperialism and that is exactly what the press did.

Songsheet cover, 1876

JINGOISM AND THE MUSIC HALLS

What was Jingoism?

In 1878, Disraeli had sent a British fleet to the Straits to protect Turkey from Russian aggression. A wave of anti-Russian public opinion had already swept Britain and the mood was reflected in the music hall song *By Jingo*, written by G. W. Hunt. One verse sums up the essence of jingoism:

We don't want to fight, but by jingo, if we do,
We've got the ships; we've got the men, and got the money too.
*We've fought **the Bear** before, and while we're Britons true,*
The Russians shall not have Constantinople.

Jingoism was a type of arrogant patriotism that sought to display Britain's military power regardless of the costs. For jingoists, it was true patriotism through which Britain would protect its interests and not allow Britain's honour and national pride to be undermined by foreign states. It was not, initially, directly linked to imperialism but it quickly came into common usage and was often directed as a term of abuse against pro-imperialists. The fact that this term had emerged through a music hall song widened its popularity. The sentiments in the song could easily be transferred to Britain's colonial expansion. Jingoism was an example of a simple idea that caught the public's imagination by presenting Britain as a country who was not afraid of its enemies.

The Music Halls: encouraging jingoism?

These were the core of popular entertainment in the late nineteenth century. Very few towns did not have at least one music hall and performers often roused their audiences with patriotic songs. It was common to have mass audience participation and patriotic songs were a perfect vehicle for this.

Again, there was no concerted effort to generate support for imperialism through the music halls but there was no doubt that the music halls did heighten popular support. The performances were colourful and often dressed in military uniforms. Many members of the audience had relatives in the army and were easily susceptible to this form of imperialist propaganda. Opportunities for entertainment were limited in the late nineteenth century and therefore the music halls became a major provider of popular entertainment. People often went to them at least once a week and so there was regular pro-imperialist propaganda available. Popular **music hall stars** emerged and the public made a real effort to see them.

The performances included many of the classic elements of pro-imperialist propaganda. Soldiers were the heroic defenders of the empire, the natives were heathens who foolishly resisted the help Britain offered, Britain was powerful, all good Britons backed their lads in the colonies, and so on.

THE CHURCH: ENTHUSIASTIC SUPPORTERS OF IMPERIALISM?

The Church provided a regular opportunity for imperialist propaganda to be distributed widely, particularly amongst the middle class. The Church promoted the idea that a fundamental element of imperial occupation was the spreading of the Christian faith. The two were in tandem.

A motivating force behind imperialism was the urge to spread Christianity. A flood of missionary societies developed, such as the United Society for the Propagation of the Gospel. These conducted fund-raising activities and lectures and so kept the positive aspects of imperialism alive. Missionaries were drawn from all sectors of society. **Mary Slessor** is a good example of a nineteenth-century female missionary in Africa.

WHY DID SOME PEOPLE REJECT POPULAR IMPERIALISM?

Not until the outbreak of the second Boer War in 1899 was there any politically significant development of

KEY PEOPLE

Music hall stars Harry Lauder (1870-1950) was a highly successful music hall star, well-known for singing his own lyrics, such as 'Roamin' in the Gloamin". Another very popular figure who had a brief but illustrious career was Dan Leno (1860-1904). In 1901 he was the first music hall performer to give a command performance before the King, Edward VII. One of the best known female music hall stars was Marie Lloyd (1870-1922). She was one of the most popular performers, made famous by songs such as 'The boy I love sits up in the Gallery' and 'My Old Man said follow the Van'.

KEY PERSON

Mary Slessor (1848–1915) Mary Slessor was from a working-class background and went to carry out her mission in Africa. She was particularly keen to end tribal customs which she regarded as unchristian. These included human sacrifice, slavery and other forms of brutality. She spent ten years on the Niger coast, interspersed with lecturing in England. What was significant was that when she died in 1915, she was given a magnificent funeral in London. Schools and official buildings flew flags at half-mast, such was her popularity.

anti-imperialism. Before this, the Liberal Party had been divided over its support for imperialism. Some liberals endorsed the Gladstonian tradition of avoiding reckless foreign adventures directed at colonial expansionism. For many liberals there was the moral issue of using force to spread British international power. Considerable anti-imperialist reaction followed the brutal suppression of the revolt of the Matabele in Rhodesia in 1893–4 during which Cecil Rhodes stated his intention of 'thoroughly thrashing the natives and giving them an everlasting lesson'.

Some liberals also questioned the economic advantages of empire. The empire encouraged preferential trade arrangements between Britain and its colonies. In turn, many liberals felt this undermined international free trade, the basis, they believed, of prosperity.

Many members of the newly emerging Socialist movement led by **Keir Hardie** strongly challenged imperialism. Hardie feared that support of popular imperialism amongst the working classes would distract them from the real issues of wages and working conditions. He was convinced that capitalists and industrialists were using patriotism and militarism to divert the working class from challenging the social and economic status quo of 1890s Britain. The high watermark of anti-imperialism came with the second Boer War and this graphically illustrates the scale of opposition that had developed by 1902.

WHAT WAS THE IMPACT OF THE SECOND BOER WAR?

Some events during the war suggested that there was widespread support for bringing the Boers under control. In May 1900, the British garrison at Mafeking was relieved after a lengthy Boer siege. There were nationwide celebrations and a new verb, to 'maffick' (meaning to celebrate wildly), came into being. The 1900 general election, the so-called 'Khaki Election', resulted in a Conservative victory and a continuance of Conservative rule. It appeared as if popular support lay with the government that had taken Britain into a war against the Boers. Despite this evidence, there was considerable opposition to imperialism illustrated and explained by the following points.

- There was considerable media coverage of the brutality of the war. Boer families were herded into concentration camps and about 110,000 civilians were in these at the end of the war. There were about 22,000 British wounded and over 5000 killed. The extensive international opposition to Britain's methods weakened support for imperialism at home.

British dead after the Battle of Spioenkop, January 1900

- Many working-class voters rejected pro-war candidates in the 1900 election. The Conservatives polled only 400,000 more votes nationally than the Liberals, from a total of 4,500,000.
- Many working-class men volunteered for military service not because they wished to show their patriotism and support for Britain's empire in its hour of need, but because they faced unemployment and poverty at home and the army was a way out of this.

The overall impact of international criticism and the brutality of the war discredited imperialism within the Liberal Party. It was of some importance that during the Boer War it was white settlers of European origins who were the victims of British aggressive imperialism and not the usual coloured African natives. By 1902, there were only a handful of Liberal imperialists left, but among them were many of the Party's leading figures such as Grey and Asquith. Political consensus between the major parties on the 'new imperialism' had evaporated with the impact of the Boer War. Many within the general public still backed imperialism, but the notion that there was universal support across all the social classes is misleading. Amongst the middle classes, imperialism was intact, but the working

Henry Campbell-Bannerman (1836-1908)
A Scot who was Liberal MP for Stirling during the years 1868 to 1908. He held a number of government posts and was Secretary for War between 1892 and 1895. From 1899 he was Liberal leader until he died in 1908. He maintained a firm anti-government line throughout the Boer War. From 1905 until 1908 he was the Liberal Prime Minister.

class had other priorities that influenced their attitudes. This process of change gained increasing momentum under the influence of the newly created Labour Party. The Liberal leader, **Henry Campbell-Bannerman**, led the opposition against the governments methods during the Boer War. He referred to these as 'methods of barbarism'.

SUMMARY QUESTIONS

1 Explain why popular literature and the music halls contributed so effectively towards making imperialism popular between 1880 and 1902.

2 'There must have been a coordinated attempt to promote imperialist propaganda to have captured the hearts and minds of so many of the general public.' How far do you agree with this view?

3 'The main reason imperialism was popular at the end of the nineteenth century was because Joseph Chamberlain was its champion.' How far do you agree with this view?

CHAPTER 6

Did Britain remain a great power between 1918 and 1939?

WHAT WAS THE IMPACT OF THE GREAT WAR?

What was the economic impact of the war?

International trade

While Britain concentrated on the war effort, its commercial rivals concentrated on seizing British markets, particularly in India, the Far East and Latin America. Britain's **staple industries** were dependent upon exports and these were the industries that suffered most from the new trading patterns caused by the war.

Between 1913 and 1918, Japanese cotton textile production grew by 55 per cent. Japan's share of the textile trade with China between 1913 and 1929 rose from twenty per cent to 26 per cent, while Britain's trade during the same period fell from 16.5 per cent to 9.55 per cent. Similarly, Japan's share of the Indian import trade rose from one per cent to 21 per cent between 1913 and 1918. This pattern of Japanese expansion and British decline continued throughout the interwar years. Japan replaced Britain as the world's leading exporter of cotton textiles.

The table below illustrates the fate of Britain's staple industries during the interwar period. The figures record the value of the exports and the percentage they represent of Britain's total exports.

	Textiles		Iron and steel		Coal	
	£m	%	£m	%	£m	%
1910–19	200.2	40	62.9	12	50	10
1920–9	288.9	37	96.5	12	65.2	8
1930–8	106	24	54.1	12	37.7	9

Shipping showed a similar pattern. Before 1914, the **carrying trade** had been dominated by Britain. During the war, the USA became the main supplier of raw materials,

> **KEY TERM**
>
> **Staple industries** Old established industries such as textiles, coal, iron and steel, and shipbuilding.

> **KEY TERM**
>
> **Carrying trade** The merchant shipping used to transport any country's exports and imports around the world.

food, and merchant shipping to Britain and its allies, and after the war Britain never recovered its 1914 position.

New production methods used in shipbuilding enabled the USA to overtake Britain as the world's largest producer of merchant shipping. Between 1909 and 1913, Britain produced 58.7% of world tonnage. By 1923 this figure was 44.7%.

Debt

The rising costs of fighting the war forced Britain to borrow money from the USA. By the end of the war, Britain had borrowed almost $4000 million, some of which had been loaned on to European allies. In effect, Britain had become a debtor nation dependent upon the USA. This was to continue throughout the interwar years as Britain's **National Debt** grew and inflation became more severe. The inflation was partly brought about because Britain increased the quantity of money in circulation in order to finance the borrowing from the USA.

The gold standard

The value of the pound was linked to gold. This was referred to as **the gold standard**. In 1914, Britain withdrew from the gold standard but returned to it in 1925. The value of the pound was set, in 1925, at $4.85, which left the pound overvalued by about ten per cent. As a result, it became more difficult for British industry to compete in international markets. Quite simply, by 1925, British goods were too expensive which discouraged many countries from importing them.

What conclusions can be drawn about the economic impact of the First World War on Britain's international status? One of the key factors necessary to enable a state to exercise international influence and project its power on a global basis was economic wealth. After 1918, the balance of international economic power had shifted away from Europe and the European great powers towards the USA. The USA became a creditor nation, the principal source of lending and the main source of raw materials.

The war had accelerated a process of economic decline in Britain but it was not the sole cause of this decline. Britain was by no means an irrelevant force in international affairs

KEY TERMS

National Debt The government borrows money to supplement revenue raised through taxes. The unpaid money is the financial debt that the nation owes to the lenders.

The gold standard The financial system whereby the world's leading industrial nations linked their currencies to the value of gold. This meant that the exchange rates between these currencies remained fixed. The gold standard maintained stability amongst the values of different currencies.

after 1918, but its capacity to use its economic wealth to reinforce its international status had been severely undermined.

What was the military and strategic impact of the war?

Military

There was a rapid de-escalation of the size of the British army after 1918.

November 1918	3,779,825 soldiers
November 1919	888,952 soldiers
November 1922	231,062 soldiers

Was this reduction the result of Britain's inability to fund a large army, and is it an indicator of increased decline as a great power?

Britain's army planners regarded the First World War as an exceptional phenomenon that would not be repeated in the future. Their view was that the army must revert to its pre-war role. This meant acting as an imperial police force, and a relatively small force could fulfil this role. Nor was it necessary to modernise the army through **increased mechanisation** because this was irrelevant to the role the army was to fulfil. Consequently, the army stagnated. Its leaders during the 1920s and 1930s were from a generation of pre-1918 career officers who were more interested in getting horses for the cavalry regiments than expanding tank units. Expenditure on modern equipment was unnecessary to protect the empire and maintain peace within it.

The British navy was no longer faced with the threat from German naval expansion after 1918. However, the French, American and Japanese fleets were expanding. In 1919, the navy tried desperately to keep its 38 battleships, 68 cruisers and 32 destroyers – there was no question of expansion. As with the army, naval planners failed to display any vision that would maintain Britain's global naval supremacy. The aircraft carrier was rejected in favour of more heavily armed battleships. Naval development was constrained by two factors.

KEY TERM

Increased mechanisation
Had the government decided to modernise the army through increased mechanisation, it would have meant an expansion in tanks, armoured vehicles and general purpose military vehicles for example.

1 Between 1919 and 1921, naval funding fell from £334 million to £84 million

2 International pressure opposed the development of a **naval arms race**. This was most clearly illustrated at **the Washington Conference** in 1921.

Strategic

The war had undoubtedly weakened or destroyed Britain's great power rivals.

- Germany was defeated, its military strength destroyed at Versailles, its empire dismantled and its economy in ruins. However, Germany could, and did, recover. Germany's resentment at its treatment at Versailles was the best possible incentive for it to rise again and restore its military and economic power.
- Russia was in the throes of revolution by 1918 but it remained a potential threat. **Lenin** declared in 1919 that no power on earth could 'hold back the progress of the world communist revolution towards the world Soviet Republic'. India, lynchpin of Britain's empire, was geographically close to Russia and therefore any instability in Russia could impact on India.

Other nations were also emerging as significant power bases.

- Japan had ambitions for imperial expansion in the Pacific and the Far East. Economic necessity, weak neighbours and aggressive military leadership drove the idea of expansionism. Britain's Far Eastern empire was vulnerable.
- The USA, although a close ally of Britain, had emerged from the war as a major economic competitor. The USA was isolationist and had no clear plan to expand its global influence but it certainly was developing the economic might to enable it to do so in the future.

For Britain, the interwar years were characterised by economic problems, military decline and the resurgence of international rivals. The First World War did not mark the irreversible retreat of Britain as a great power, but it did accelerate debilitating weaknesses from which Britain could hardly recover. Restoration of the supremacy it had enjoyed in the nineteenth century was highly unlikely. Another potential problem was resurfacing in a more threatening form after 1918. This was the issue of rising nationalism within the British Empire.

What was the impact of rising nationalism in the Empire?

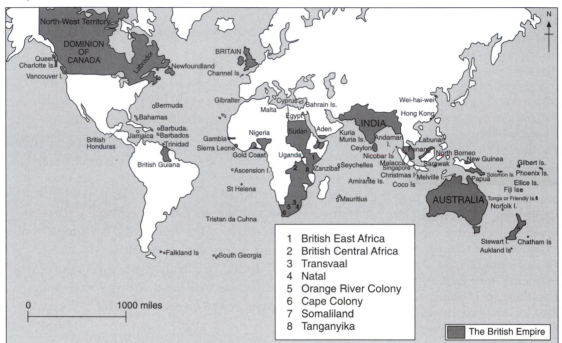

1 British East Africa
2 British Central Africa
3 Transvaal
4 Natal
5 Orange River Colony
6 Cape Colony
7 Somaliland
8 Tanganyika

The British Empire

The extent of the British Empire in 1918

Nationalism within the British Empire was not a consequence of the First World War. It was a long-term phenomenon that, like Britain's economic decline, was merely accelerated by the war.

Indian nationalism
The demand for independence had begun in earnest with the formation of the **Indian National Congress** in 1885. During the First World War, Indian citizens had rallied to the imperial cause. Increasingly, however, nationalist groups demanded reform as the cost of India's continued participation in the war. By 1917, the British government was willing to move towards some form of self-government in India, but within the framework of the empire. In 1935 Britain introduced a further Government of India Act:

* elected Indians were to determine policy on public health, education and agriculture

KEY ORGANISATION

Indian National Congress
This was founded in 1885. Initially it was not opposed to British rule in India. This position changed over time as the Congress became very active in the Indian Nationalist Movement. Under the leadership of Gandhi it campaigned for non-violent non-cooperation with the British rulers in India.

- this was to happen at provincial level rather than on a nationwide basis
- the Viceroy was to control foreign policy, defence, law and order, and financial policy.

This measure failed to satisfy Indian nationalists. A policy of passive resistance was promoted by the Indian National Congress Party and one of its leading figures, **Mahatma Gandhi**.

In 1929, the Viceroy, Lord Irwin, announced that it was Britain's intention to grant India dominion status. This was not enough for the Congress Party and Gandhi continued with his policy of civil disobedience. Clearly the British government was willing to accept some significant form of reform and Gandhi was convinced that he could achieve more than merely dominion status.

In 1935, Britain introduced the Government of India Act. This aimed at the creation of a federation or union of Indian states, each becoming responsible for its own internal affairs through a series of provincial parliaments. There would be an elected national parliament but the British Viceroy would remain overall head of state and as such remain in control of foreign policy and defence. Britain had still not committed itself to the idea of independence for India. As Gandhi commented on the 1935 Act, 'India is still a prison, but the superintendent allows the prisoners to elect the officers who run the jail.'

The dominions
Nationalism was less clearly defined amongst the white controlled dominion states of the empire. However, there was a powerful post-war drive amongst the dominions to redefine their relationship with Britain.

The key issue was the demand to have control over their own foreign policies and to be recognised as sovereign states in their own right. Britain attempted to bow to this demand for clarity in the status of the dominions in 1926 at the Imperial Conference. The conference agreed to what was known as the Balfour Declaration.

KEY PERSON

Mahatma (Mohandas Karamchand) Gandhi (1869–1948) Gandhi was born into a wealthy merchant family and educated in Britain where he qualified as a lawyer. Whilst working in South Africa in 1893, he began a successful passive resistance campaign against white South African discrimination against Indians. In 1915, he returned to India and became a leading figure in the Indian National Congress Party and the Nationalist movement. He promoted the ideas of non-violent civil disobedience in order to make British rule in India impossible. He also advocated self-reliance and the non-importation of British manufactured goods. Gandhi was able to appeal to the Indian masses and disrupt British rule through them.

The Declaration stated that the dominions were:

autonomous communities within the British Empire, equal in status, in no way subordinate to one another in any respect of their domestic or external affairs, though united by a common allegiance to the Crown, freely associated as members of the British Commonwealth of nations.

The Balfour Declaration recognised a reality that already existed. The dominions were already self-governing and they were willing to consider breaking away from close ties with Britain unless the final act of independent status, the right to exercise an independent foreign policy, was granted by Britain. The final act of redefinition of the relationship came in 1931 with the Statute of Westminster. This gave the dominions the right to change their own constitutions without consulting Britain. They were not automatically to be bound by British law. The dominions were now voluntary members of a commonwealth of states but independent nations in their own right.

The Middle East

Britain's influence in this area had increased after 1918 when the Turkish Empire was dismembered and Britain assumed control of a number of **mandated territories** from the Turks in addition to the states it already controlled as part of the empire. The whole area became increasingly unstable during the interwar years.

- Iraq, Trans-Jordan and Egypt – In 1920, revolts threatened British control of its mandate in Iraq. As Colonial Secretary in 1921, Winston Churchill's priority was to ensure that British influence in Iraq remained intact. The route to achieve this was to back a new pro-British Iraqi leader, **Faisal**, and to grant Iraq independence with the condition that during the life of the mandate British military bases would remain. In effect, Iraq remained a close ally of Britain's and British influence was guaranteed through cooperative local leadership. Ironically, before the British backed Faisal as King of Iraq he had been one of the leaders of the Arab revolts of 1916–19. Britain established a similar arrangement with regard to Trans-Jordan by installing Faisal's brother, Abdullah, as ruler.

KEY TERM

Autonomous communities States free to govern themselves without any external control.

KEY TERM

Mandated territories The Turkish Empire in the Middle East was dismantled after the First World War. Britain and France took control of these territories in 1919, not as permanent parts of their own empires, but on a temporary basis until they could become self-governing. This power of control was the mandate. Britain was mandated to govern Palestine, Trans-Jordan and Iraq.

KEY PERSON

Faisal (1885–1933) He was King of Iraq from 1921 until his death in 1933. He was installed in that job by the British and he laid the foundations for Iraq's independence.

Faced with serious nationalist demonstrations in 1919, Britain recognised Egyptian independence in 1922. As in Iraq, this was a compromise because Britain retained control of Egypt's foreign and defence policies. In 1936, the Anglo–Egyptian Treaty gave Egypt control over its own army but ensured that a large British military presence remained to protect British interests in the Suez Canal zone.

- Palestine – In 1917, Britain had promised support for a Jewish state but the details of its extent and structure were vague. Palestine was strategically important to British interests in the Middle East because it defended the eastern flank of the Suez Canal, a vital link between Britain and its Far Eastern Empire. Britain faced a massive anti-Jewish reaction by Palestinian Arabs, particularly in the face of ever increasing Jewish immigration. Britain never managed to establish a satisfactory compromise between the Jews and the Arabs, although its policy did favour Arab interests. By 1939 Jewish immigration had been significantly limited in order to maintain Arab support in this vital region. Arab oil was essential to Britain and alienating Palestinian Arabs could be damaging to wider British interests in the region.

- Other dependencies – There was little interest in nationalism in the rest of the empire and therefore there was little pressure on Britain to consider any form of limited self-government. Despite this, as in other parts of the empire, British rule was very dependent upon the cooperation of local leaders and loyal local people to act as security forces and administrators.

Were there any changes in Britain's imperial policy?

An indicator of Britain's decline as a great power might be considered to be its inability after 1918 to resist nationalism and the demand for independence within the empire with any degree of success. Equally, there might be some evidence of a general retreat from empire, as the cost of war and Britain's inability to maintain a large military presence on a global basis made the loss of the British Empire inevitable.

What is important to understand about the relationship Britain had with its empire in the interwar years is that there was no uniform approach. The empire was diverse in its nature and Britain had differing needs and interests from the states that made up the empire. Britain's response to the problems within the empire was as diverse as the different parts of the empire.

Britain's relationship with its empire

- By 1919, the dominions were already almost self-governing. If Britain was to retain a positive relationship with these strategically and economically important allies, it had to move towards independence within the framework of a Commonwealth relationship. This was a development that Britain could not resist but it should not necessarily be seen as indicative of Britain's decline as a great power after 1918. It made eminent sense for Britain to retain these states as friends and this could only be achieved by formally accepting the reality of independence.

- India was in a different position. The First World War had drained Britain economically. Overseas investments and trade had been fundamentally damaged. The costs of maintaining the administration in a colony the size of India were prohibitive. A lack of political agreement and the determination of some British politicians to reject any form of independence for India prevented a compromise. Indian nationalism was more developed and more sophisticated than nationalism in any other part of the empire. There was recognition that some form of national freedom would have to be accepted. This process had already started before 1914.

- Strategically, Britain could not allow its influence in the Middle East to be damaged. As with the dominions, the route to protecting British interests was to form a positive relationship with the states. Britain's tactic was to grant some form of independence but ensure British influence remained intact. Granting Iraq independence, for example, was not an indicator of Britain's decline through an inability to govern. Rather it was a sound political and diplomatic move, which ensured British dominance in the vital region of the Middle East and removed the problem of containing ongoing nationalist revolts. An almost identical position applied to Britain's relationship with Egypt.

- Clearly Britain had moved on from its nineteenth-century concept of imperial exploitation. After 1918, Britain adopted a more pragmatic and realistic view of its relationship with the empire. What had not changed was Britain's determination to use the empire to Britain's economic and strategic advantage and that meant recognising the reality that nationalism would not simply go away. A more positive relationship had to be established if British interests were to be protected. None of this suggests that Britain was losing the empire because of the effects of the First World War. Britain remained committed to the idea that it was better to use rather than to lose its empire.

Appeasement: The death throes of a great power?

Here, we need to look at whether or not **appeasement** was indicative of Britain's decline as a great power. Appeasement was not the only option open to British policy-makers. Other choices included:

- greater commitment to international cooperation through the League of Nations
- the formation of an international alliance system committed to containing the aggressive nationalism of Germany, Italy and Japan.

The question then becomes why did Britain not adopt an alternative policy? Was it because it was too weak to consider such alternatives?

- Popular opinion was profoundly against another war. The government had to respond to this popular view.
- Economically, Britain was in no position to consider a policy that might lead to war. The economic crisis left by the First World War deepened after the international economic collapse of 1929.
- Although Britain's empire was larger after 1918, and therefore Britain was apparently stronger as a global power, this strength was more apparent than real. Britain's resources were barely at a level to ensure the protection of this growing empire. Unity within the imperial family was simply not there. Given these

internal problems, Britain was not in a position to adopt an aggressive stance towards maintaining international peace. There was, too, no absolute certainty that the whole of Britain's empire would rally round the mother country in a time of international crisis. National self-interest amongst the white dominions reduced the certainty of imperial unity upon which Britain might depend in any future war.

- Militarily, Britain was profoundly weakened. Although a rearmament programme was introduced from 1937, this came too late to contain the expansionist policies of Germany, Italy and Japan. Britain was simply not ready for a war in 1939 and therefore had to promote a policy that would do everything possible to prevent the outbreak of war.
- The process of international cooperation based on the League of Nations had failed. Britain had to pursue a policy that was independent of international cooperation. This was made all the more urgent by the failure of the French to adopt an internationalist view. France was only interested in its own security and that was to be achieved through a form of isolationism.
- Britain knew that its vital sea lane communications, which serviced the empire and trade, would be difficult to defend.

Overall, Britain's weakened state after the First World War did contribute significantly to the policy of appeasement. However, it is important to recognise that there were other options open to Britain and these clearly indicate that Britain's status as a great power was still intact.

Britain remained a great power in the interwar years but a power that had been profoundly but not terminally weakened.

SUMMARY QUESTIONS

1 'The most important threat to Britain's great power status between the wars lay in the problems it faced within the empire.' How far do you agree with this view?

2 To what extent could Britain claim to be a great power after 1918?

CHAPTER 7

Did Britain's foreign and imperial policies change after 1945?

The British government's foreign and imperial policies after 1945 were characterised by the need to adapt to new international, strategic and economic circumstances, while maintaining a degree of continuity.

WHAT WAS THE ECONOMIC IMPACT OF THE SECOND WORLD WAR?

- Armaments had been at the very centre of Britain's wartime expenditure. Even before the outbreak of war in 1939 Britain had already been forced to increase public spending on a rearmament programme. In 1933, Britain's defence spending stood at about £100 million, which was the equivalent of three per cent of Britain's **gross national product** (GNP). By 1945, government expenditure had risen to £6.1 billion. There was a massive increase in productivity between 1938 and 1944. This increase earned nothing for Britain since it was focused entirely on the production of war materials. By 1944, the war was costing Britain half of its GNP.
- Britain did not have sufficient wealth to finance the war without some form of external aid. That additional support came through government borrowing. Britain borrowed money directly, but during the Second World War, a new form of borrowing was introduced. This was the **lend lease** scheme. By 1945, Britain owed about £3 billion to its overseas creditors.

The economic crisis had worsened through the collapse of international trade. This had the effect of seriously damaging Britain's invisible earnings. These had been a vital element in enabling Britain to maintain a favourable balance of payments position. By 1945, Britain faced a balance of payments deficit of £875 million.

The economic crisis deepened still further on 17 August 1945 when the USA abruptly ended the lend lease scheme.

KEY TERM

Gross national product
The annual value of Britain's earnings.

KEY AGREEMENT

Lend lease, 1941–5 From 1941, the USA agreed to provide Britain with war materials. This system operated like a form of credit, although Britain was not required to make any repayments until the war ended. In total, Britain received about $30 million worth of goods. This contributed significantly to the debt Britain was left with when the war ended.

Britain's military costs continued because it was forced to maintain occupation troops in Germany. Growing fears of Russian expansionism also heightened the need for Britain's military presence in Europe.

American financial aid was essential to help Britain's post-war economic adjustment. Borrowing created dependency and this was to have a significant impact on Britain's international policy-making after 1945. By the autumn of 1945, the USA offered to reduce the lend lease debt to $650 million, a fraction of its real size. An additional loan of $3.75 billion at two per cent interest was also offered. In return for this financial package, the USA demanded that Britain ratify the 1944 **Bretton Woods** agreement.

ANGLO–AMERICAN RELATIONS, 1945–63

Britain and the USA had long been allies, but during the interwar period, the USA had pursued a policy of self-imposed isolation from international affairs. America's role in the war was crucial to victory and the war determined that the USA would abandon its isolationist policies for good. Anglo–American relations may be considered in two distinct phases.

1945–57: A stronger relationship with the USA?

Conditions in 1945 made it almost impossible for Britain not to cultivate a strong relationship with the USA:

- the war had financially drained Britain
- the USA was economically and militarily the strongest international power
- Britain was heavily in debt to the USA
- imperial problems in India heightened Britain's international problems
- the spread of communism across Eastern Europe convinced Britain that Europe as a whole was under ideological and military threat from the Soviet Union
- the states of Western Europe had been as badly damaged as Britain during the war and were in an equally weakened state and unable to defend themselves against a Soviet threat.

There was no doubt that Britain regarded a firm alliance with the USA as central to the defence of Britain, and

Bretton Woods, 1944
Twenty-eight countries, including Britain, agreed to establish an International Monetary Fund (IMF) and a World Bank. The IMF was meant to keep the exchange rates between currencies stable. The World Bank was there to provide loans that would fund major developments in member states.

indeed the whole of Western Europe. The USA was less committed to the idea of an Atlantic alliance and in early 1946 still favoured some degree of isolationism. British policy aimed to draw the USA into such an alliance.

The withdrawal from Greece in 1947 illustrates British thinking towards the USA. There was an urgent need to cut military spending. Britain had been supporting anti-communist forces during the **Greek Civil War**, but this ended on 31 March 1947. Almost immediately **Truman** ask the US Congress to replace British aid to Greece in their struggle against communism. The Truman Doctrine and, by June 1947, the Marshall Plan were underway. The Anglo–American relationship culminated in the creation of **NATO** in 1949.

Britain's support for the USA in the Korean War was partly the result of the need to back its principal ally, but also because Britain perceived the spread of communism in the Far East as a growing threat to British imperial possessions there. Britain was already facing problems in Malaya. In addition, Britain still wanted to preserve some degree of independence from US influence. The most obvious method was to develop its own nuclear weapons programme. By 1952, Britain had its own long-range bomber nuclear strike force, although it continued to lag well behind the nuclear expansion of the USA.

Britain's determination to pursue policies independently of the USA was also revealed in the Suez Crisis (1956). When Nasser nationalised the canal, Britain used military force to restore its own control and prestige. The USA rejected the use of militarism and they feared the risk it posed in terms of forcing Egypt into an alignment with the Soviet Union. US Cold War interests were at stake and Britain's actions were threatening them. The incident illustrated Britain's inability to influence events in the Middle East and the growing dependency on the USA.

1957–64: Closer to the USA or stand-alone?
The Suez affair had damaged Anglo–American relations. The reconstruction and strengthening of this Atlantic alliance became an essential objective in British foreign policy thinking from 1957. The key issue here is why did Britain move towards a closer alliance with the USA rather

than developing its own position as a global power or strengthening its alliance with other European powers to create a strong regional alliance?

In April 1957, Macmillan's government issued its thinking on Britain's defence strategy in a White Paper, *Defence: Outline of Future Policy*. The economic costs of maintaining a large conventional army and the fact that nuclear technology was rapidly making such forces obsolete moved the government to focus on Britain's nuclear capability. Equally, Britain could not act as a main player in the international **nuclear arms race**, therefore the logical position for Britain was to align itself more firmly to the USA's nuclear might while at the same time having enough nuclear capability to serve as a deterrent against attack.

In March 1957, Harold Macmillan agreed to 60 Thor intermediate range ballistic missiles being stationed in Britain. This was the latest technology and it had no financial cost for Britain. Although Britain had the ability to maintain nuclear warheads, what it did not have was an effective missile delivery system for these weapons. By 1962, Macmillan had secured the US Polaris missile system, a submarine launched system. This reinforced the fact that Britain's defence systems were heavily dependent upon US technology and US finance. At the heart of Britain's growing alliance with the USA was Britain's inability to finance its own independent nuclear capability.

ANGLO–EUROPEAN RELATIONS, 1945–63

Britain regarded the security of Western Europe as an integral part of its own security. Two issues may be considered in order to understand the nature of Anglo–European relations in terms of British foreign policy.

The 'German Question': a central element of British policy?

The Potsdam Conference produced a plan for the short-term future of Germany but nothing was decided about Germany's long-term future. Occupation arrangements were made and the country was divided into four zones.

KEY TERM

Nuclear arms race The 1950s saw the build-up of nuclear weapons by the Soviet Union and the USA. The idea behind this competition was the certainty that gaining a lead was necessary for security.

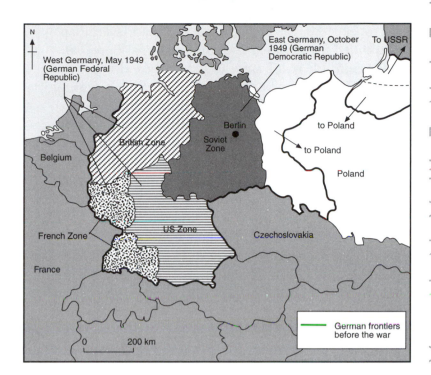

The occupation zones in Germany, 1945

KEY EVENT

Bi-zonia, 1947 The British and US occupation zones were united. The aim was to enable these areas to experience a more rapid economic recovery. A new currency was introduced into this zone.

Fears that communism might spread into the war devastated British and US zones led to the creation of **bi-zonia** on 1 January 1947.

The reconstruction of Germany became a central element of British policy in Europe. The aim was not only to prevent the spread of communism into Western Germany but also to prepare Germany for democratic reconstruction, which would align Germany to the non-communist Western powers. The Soviet Union was pursuing a similar pro-communist line towards Eastern Germany.

European integration: viable option for Britain?

Britain's transatlantic alliance system with the USA was part of a wider strategy to enable Britain to maintain a great power role in the post-war world. The question was could closer links with Europe also play a part in this objective of enhancing Britain's global power base or was the USA the only strand in the achievement of this aim?

In January 1949, the Foreign Office summed up British policy:

Our policy should be to assist Europe as far as we can...In no circumstances must we assist them beyond the point at which the assistance leaves us too weak to be a worthwhile ally for the USA.

In October 1950, the French produced the Pleven Plan, which called for an integrated, multinational European army responsible to a European Assembly and Defence Minister. This was to be the European Defence Community (EDC). This form of European integration was dismissed by Attlee as 'unworkable and unsound'. Britain continued to refuse to take part in the EDC because a greater European commitment might undermine Britain's other global responsibilities, particularly the importance that Britain placed on its relationship with the Commonwealth. However, the USA wanted Germany to rearm and the EDC to succeed because this would show that Europe was contributing to its own security and was not totally dependent on the USA. Britain feared that the USA might return to isolationism if Europe did not respond positively.

BRITAIN AND THE EMPIRE

It appeared, immediately after the war, that Britain was preparing to abandon the empire. The creation of an independent India and Pakistan in August 1947 was followed, in January 1948, by independence for Burma. In May, Britain evacuated Palestine. The costs of holding on to these parts of the empire outweighed the advantages. However, elsewhere, the empire still had a very significant role to play in Britain's determination to function as a global power. Britain was determined not to submit to what appeared to be the USA's objective of turning Britain into a European power.

The post-war Labour government was certainly committed to developing the role of the empire in the process of keeping Britain a global power. In January 1948, the Foreign Secretary, Ernest Bevin, identified the basis of British policy towards the empire.

> *Provided we can organise a Western European alliance…it should be possible to develop our own power and influence equal to that of the USA and the USSR. We have the material resources in the colonial empire, if we develop them.*

The Commonwealth: how was it to be used?

One way of achieving Bevin's aim was through the Commonwealth. In the interwar period, the Commonwealth had been regarded as the 'white dominions'. After the war there was the real possibility that

KEY ALLIANCE

ANZUS, 1951–4 This is an acronym for Australia, New Zealand and the US. It is otherwise known as the Pacific Security Treaty which was a military alliance formed in 1951. It was replaced in 1954 by the South East Asia Treaty Organisation (SEATO).

KEY TERMS

Sterling area States that held the British pound as their reserve currency. The system was designed, in part, to maintain the value of the pound against other currencies, especially the US dollar.

British mandate Britain was to administer and govern Palestine and act as its protector until such times as self-government became possible. The mandate system ensured that Britain could not absorb it into its empire.

Zionism This called for the creation of a Jewish homeland in Palestine, the biblical land of Zion. This Zionist state would be called Israel. Inevitably, some of the land that would form part of the new Israel was inhabited by Arabs who were not prepared to give up their control of land they saw as theirs. Zionists were willing to use violence to achieve their objectives.

Arab nationalism This was a movement that aimed to create independent Arab states in the Middle East. Some Arab nationalists also aimed at a regional Arab 'super-state' in the Middle East.

the Commonwealth would break up as Ireland and Burma refused to join. The Commonwealth remained fragile as Australia and New Zealand joined the USA in the **ANZUS**. Britain wanted to use the Commonwealth as a union of states that would continue to offer some protection to Britain, and each other, and offer Britain strategic advantages on a global level.

Colonial economic development

After 1945, Britain had a powerful motive to develop its dependent territories since imperial products were major dollar earners. Malaya, for example, provided over half of the USA's rubber imports and almost all of its tin. This earned around $170 million annually. The **sterling area** arrangements meant that Britain bought up the dollars and credited them against sterling which prevented countries like Malaya using dollars outside the sterling area. In effect, Britain's colonial dependencies were exploited. Any developments were designed to enhance the earning potential of the colonies and thus strengthen Britain's economic position against the USA.

The Middle East

Britain's position in the Middle East was driven by economic priorities after 1945. Britain controlled the oil production of Iran, the Middle East's largest oil producer. Protection of these resources was vital to Britain's industrial and economic development. In 1951, the refineries were nationalised and the British were forced out. In 1953, British and American intelligence agencies overthrew the Iranian leadership and restored British interests, albeit now shared with the USA who were able to demand a share in the oil revenues. This incident reveals Britain's determination to maintain some economic advantage through its foreign connections.

PALESTINE, 1947–8

Britain's involvement in Palestine began at the end of the First World War. Formerly part of the Turkish Empire, Palestine became a **British mandate** and almost immediately became a problem for Britain because of the clashes between **Zionism** and **Arab nationalism**. Britain's approach to this conflict was to recognise the Zionist claim to a Jewish homeland but also to guarantee the civil and religious rights of the Arabs in Palestine. It was a compromise that solved nothing. British attempts to create a partitioned Palestine in 1937 failed as neither the Jews nor the Arabs were willing to compromise.

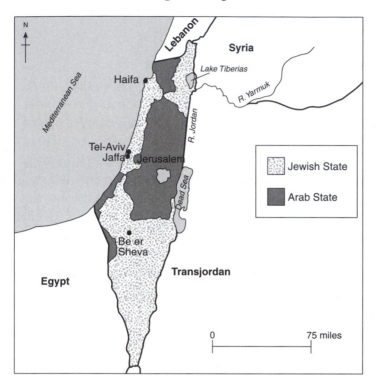

The planned Partition of Palestine, 1947 – UN General Assembly Resolution 181

1947–8: Why did Britain abandon its mandate in Palestine?

In April 1947, the British government asked for the 'Question of Palestine' to be placed on the agenda of **the United Nations** General Assembly. A special committee was convened to prepare proposals for the area's future. On 29 November 1947, the General Assembly voted to adopt the committee's recommendations for partition of Palestine into a Jewish and an Arab state. On 14 May 1948, the state of Israel proclaimed its independence. The key issue here is why did Britain abandon its mandate in Palestine?

Economic factors

The Middle East was a vital source of oil supplies for Britain. There was a powerful argument to suggest that Britain's continued presence in Palestine would reinforce its ability to preserve some stability in the region as a whole. Conversely, there was the reality that maintaining such a

KEY ORGANISATION

The United Nations This replaced the League of Nations. It was formed in 1945. Its aim was to preserve peace and remove the causes of conflict. It played an important role in international peacekeeping throughout the period of the Cold War.

presence was prohibitively expensive. In 1946, a civil war was raging and Britain was forced to put 100,000 troops into Palestine. The annual cost was £40 million and the force was the equivalent of one British soldier for every eighteen inhabitants of Palestine. Britain was in no position, economically, to maintain such a force indefinitely. Even Churchill, an ardent supporter of British power abroad asked, 'What are they [British troops] doing there? What good are we getting out of it?'

Strategic factors

British politicians were deeply divided over the strategic significance of a British military presence in the Eastern Mediterranean. The wartime Foreign Secretary, Anthony Eden, commented in April 1945 on the crucial strategic importance of the Eastern Mediterranean in the defence of the empire when he noted that 'it is there that the empire can be cut in half'. This made a British military presence in the area 'a matter of life and death to the British Empire'. The British military establishment argued that the real threat to Britain was from Soviet aggression and the best form of defence was strategically located airbases. The military chiefs argued in 1946 that 'the threat of attack by air or long-range weapons will be our one effective military deterrent to Soviet aggression'. The rationale for retaining a British military presence in Palestine lay in its geographic location: 'The Middle East is nearest to the important Soviet industrial and oil producing areas.'

The post-war Prime Minister, Attlee, took a very different strategic view of the Eastern Mediterranean. India was on the brink of attaining independence and the era of airpower had established itself, hence the strategic importance of controlling territory had been dramatically reduced.

Diplomatic factors

The Jews held great political influence in the USA. There was a powerful Jewish lobby in Washington that promoted US support for the creation of Israel. Maintaining good relations with the USA was a vital element of post-war British foreign policy. The question was should Britain pursue its own strategic and economic interests in the Middle East or should it cooperate with US support for a Zionist state and therefore risk alienating the Arabs?

In effect, Britain's policy in Palestine was driven by a number of factors that made withdrawal the only viable option in 1948.

- It was too expensive to maintain the mandate.
- Britain's closest ally supported a Zionist state.
- Britain's strategic priorities lay in the defence of Western Europe.
- Palestine was not a British colony, therefore the spectre of decolonisation was not spreading beyond India.

In August 1947, the Chancellor of the Exchequer, Hugh Dalton, commented on Britain's response to the terrorism in Palestine: 'You cannot…have a secure base on top of a wasps' nest.' This was as good a reason as any to withdraw.

Overall, Britain's post-war foreign and imperial policies were designed partly in response to the economic impact of the war but also to ensure that Britain still had the opportunity to function as a great power even within the new superpower bi-polar world. The alliance with the USA was all-important, but not to the point where Britain was simply a puppet dancing to the USA's tune. Britain wanted to use the USA to protect Europe. It wanted to benefit from the USA's nuclear power and it wanted to use the empire to reinforce its global influence and economic strength. Europe was less significant in Britain's planning. A stronger alliance with Europe and the development of a regional European power base would not have achieved Britain's global ambitions.

SUMMARY QUESTIONS

1 Why did Britain want a strong alliance with the USA after 1945? Explain your answer.

2 Explain why economic factors were so important in British foreign and imperial policy after 1945.

3 Assess the importance of three events that illustrate Britain's aim of remaining a global power after 1945.

CHAPTER 8

How and why did Britain decolonise after 1945?

From the end of the Second World War, the British Empire began a process of terminal decline. The basic question is, was there a clear pattern to this process of decolonisation? Were there common reasons for the decolonisation or was each step in the process an individual one and specific to each individual colony?

INDIAN INDEPENDENCE, 1947: WHY DID BRITAIN GRANT INDEPENDENCE SO QUICKLY TO ITS FLAGSHIP COLONY?

India had been considered the most important of all of Britain's colonies. It was the 'jewel in the crown' and yet it was the first non-white controlled colony to be granted complete independence after the Second World War. The key issue here is why did Britain grant independence with such rapidity?

Background, 1945–7

Immediately after the war ended, a general election was held in India. The Congress Party won a resounding majority in the non-Muslim provinces. The Muslim League, led by **Mohammed Ali Jinnah**, also did well and pressed its claims for a separate Muslim state of Pakistan. Gandhi was determined that an independent India should remain united. It was rapidly becoming clear that the potential for India to collapse into a state of anarchy was increasing. Civil war was a real possibility.

In July 1946, elections for a constituent assembly were held and the Congress gained an absolute majority. Congress made it clear that a partitioned India was not going to happen. The Muslim League declared 16 August a **Direct Action Day**. Mostly this was passive resistance by Muslims, but in Calcutta bloody rioting erupted. An impossible deadlock had gripped Indian politics, as neither side was willing to compromise.

KEY PERSON

Mohammed Ali Jinnah (1876–1948) During the 1890s, Jinnah studied law in Britain. Although a Muslim, he joined the Indian National Congress Party. After a period out of politics he returned to lead the All Indian Muslim League. By the start of the Second World War, he was demanding not only independence but also the creation of a separate Muslim state of Pakistan through the partition of British India.

KEY EVENT

Direct Action Day This was a show of unity amongst Muslims in their struggle to achieve a separate and independent Muslim state.

On 20 February 1947, Attlee announced that Britain would leave India no later than June 1948. At the same time he recalled the Viceroy, Wavell, and appointed **Lord Louis Mountbatten** as the new Viceroy with responsibility for preparing for the transfer of power. Mountbatten brought the date for withdrawal forward to 15 August 1947. The deadline sharpened the minds of Congress and the Muslim League. Congress finally accepted the inevitable necessity of partition and the new state of Pakistan came into being.

Why did Britain withdraw from India when it did?

Both long and short-term factors contribute to an answer to this question. Certainly pre-war issues were highly significant. However, there was increased pressure on Britain from 1945 created by the Second World War. The new international scene became highly significant in the decolonisation process.

KEY PERSON

Lord Louis Mountbatten (1900–79) Mountbatten was an admiral and an administrator. During the Second World War, he became Commander in Chief of British forces in South East Asia. He later took the title First Earl Mountbatten of Burma. He was the last Viceroy of India and he oversaw India's transition to independence.

Mountbatten and Jinnah in New Delhi in 1947

- Before 1939, Britain promised to transfer a measure of power to India at some point in the future. This did not necessarily amount to a final commitment to Indian independence, but in practice the inclination towards independence was in place before the war began.
- The war had a damaging impact on Anglo–Indian relations. The war forced Britain to mobilise the empire's resources and India was no exception to this process. Economic controls were introduced; labour was conscripted and political rights suppressed. Congress began a 'Quit India' campaign. The war had served to heighten Indian nationalism rather than dilute it into passive patriotism. Nationalist fervour was even stronger when the war ended.
- Even before the war, India was becoming increasingly free of British control. It had its own tariff system against British goods and the 'Indianisation' of the army and the civil service was well developed. In 1939, Britain had agreed to pay all the costs of the Indian army that went beyond normal peacetime defence costs.

By 1945, Britain was in debt to India to the sum of £1.3 billion. Financially, India was becoming an economic liability rather than an imperial economic asset. India had declined as a major importer of British goods, although Britain's imports of Indian goods increased.

- In 1945, the British Labour Party took power. Ideologically, the leadership was committed to decolonisation. British popular opinion was not focused on holding on to India. The war had just ended and the prospect of sending more troops to suppress Indian nationalist violence was inconceivable to most Britons. The government had no popular mandate from the British people to struggle to keep India.

By 1945, Britain's empire was no longer serving its purpose, either economically or strategically. India was the first to achieve independence because its nationalist struggle was more advanced than most other colonies.

THE SUEZ CRISIS, 1956: A TURNING POINT IN BRITISH DECOLONISATION?

The Suez Canal Crisis has frequently been referred to as a turning point in British decolonisation. Was this defeat for Britain a central factor in accelerating decolonisation or was it only of marginal significance?

KEY PERSON

Gamal Abdel Nasser (1918–70) In 1952, Nasser was a leading figure in the bloodless removal of King Farouk as leader of Egypt. Nasser was a leading figure in the drive towards a united Arab federation in the Middle East. In 1958 he was instrumental in the creation of the United Arab Republic, which survived until 1971. He was an early and influential leader of the non-aligned Arab movement and he was determined not to commit Egypt or the Arab world to either the US-led capitalist West or the Soviet-led communist East.

Background

In 1954, **Colonel Nasser** declared himself Prime Minister and then, in 1956, President of Egypt, thereby overthrowing the rebel army officer General Neguib as head of state. Nasser's aim was the creation of a neutral bloc of Arab states under the leadership of Egypt. He had already written a clear statement of his ideas entitled *The Philosophy of Revolution* in which he called for the removal of the white man from the Middle East. For Nasser, Egypt's future lay in an alliance with other nations in Africa and even Asia. Britain regarded Nasser as a fundamental danger to its interests in the Middle East and Egypt, which it regarded as a western satellite state. British imperialism was still alive and well as far as Egypt was concerned in 1956.

Nationalisation of the Suez Canal

In July 1956, the British and French owned Suez Canal was nationalised by Nasser and declared Egyptian territory. *The*

Times editorial commented: 'If Nasser gets away with it, all the British and western interests in the Middle East will crumble.' From the very outset there was a direct link being established between the maintenance of Britain's imperial status and a successful stand being taken against Egypt.

While Britain and France prepared for war against Egypt, it was of some significance that of all the Commonwealth members only the Central African Federation (Southern and Northern Rhodesia and Nyasaland) gave unqualified support to Britain.

Britain and France colluded with the Israelis. Israel felt threatened by Egypt's support for Palestine guerrillas and seized the opportunity to attack Egypt. On 29 October 1956, Israel attacked Egypt, and Britain and France were able to enter Egypt on the pretext of acting as peacemakers in order to end the conflict. British forces arrived on 5 November and a ceasefire was declared the following day. On 29 November, faced with US pressure, Britain and France agreed to withdraw their forces as a UN peacekeeping force took over.

Anthony Eden and Colonel Nasser in Cairo a year before the Suez Crisis

Colonel Nasser being carried through Port Said after the British evacuation in 1956

Why did Britain withdraw troops?

Why did it happen and what consequences did it hold for British post-1945 imperialism?

The British Prime Minister, **Anthony Eden**, was determined to remove Nasser from power. Eden had commented to a Foreign Office official, 'But what's all this nonsense about isolating Nasser, of "neutralising" him as you call it? I want him destroyed, can't you understand?' By invading Egypt, Britain had succeeded in mobilising international opposition to what was seen as aggressive imperialism. Post-war Britain was in no position to ignore its new dependency upon the USA and the importance of the international balance of power within a **Cold War context**.

Economically, Britain was too weak to stand up to international opposition. The value of the pound fell dramatically from August 1956 and by November Britain faced an economic crisis. Britain had lost nearly half a billion pounds, the equivalent of a fifth of its financial reserves. The Chancellor, Harold Macmillan, applied to the International Monetary Fund for a $550 million loan only to be refused because of US pressure. A British MP, Angus Maude, commented that Britain had 'to admit to the world that we are now an American satellite.'

The Suez Crisis had exposed Britain's weaknesses, its economic limitations and its dependency upon the USA. In the post-war Cold War world, the British Empire was increasingly less relevant as a means of preserving Britain's economic and strategic protection. A British politician summed this up when he commented that Britain's post-war priority was 'to preserve an anti-Soviet tier of defence, and behind it quietly and with honour and dignity, reduce our commitments'. The commitments referred to were the remaining territories under British imperial rule.

It is possible to see Suez as a catalyst in British decolonisation. However, the impact of Suez should not be overstated. Britain soon restored good relations with the USA without any need to accelerate decolonisation. Also, the process of decolonisation had already begun in earnest. For example, Ghana had already been promised independence and this was granted in 1957. Nationalist movements in many African colonies also had a significant impact on moves towards decolonisation.

THE MAU MAU AND KENYA: PATERNALISTIC WHITE CONTROL?

Since the end of the nineteenth century, large numbers of white settlers had established themselves in Kenya, dominating the most fertile part of Kenya, the 'White Highlands' in the Aberdare Mountains, with their plantations. The native Africans were restricted to overcrowded tribal areas. Whites also dominated Kenyan politics by a power sharing process with the Colonial Office. Kenya was a clear example of paternalistic white control and this is how it emerged from the war in 1945.

There was no suggestion in 1945 that Britain was even remotely considering independence for Kenya. In addition to the many native tribal groups and the white settlers, there was also a large group of Asian, mainly Indian, settlers. Generally, these were prosperous business people who facilitated much of Kenya's financial and commercial activities.

In 1944, the nationalist party, the Kenyan African Union (KAU), was founded and **Jomo Kenyatta** quickly became its leader. The majority tribe, **the Kikuyu**, demanded the restoration of the White Highlands into their hands. Kenyatta was seen as a kind of Messiah who would take control and restore Kikuyu power and prosperity.

The Mau Mau

By 1949, Kikuyu discontent had coalesced into what became known as the Mau Mau. The organisation demanded the restoration of African lands to the African people. It was quickly regarded by the Kikuyu as a Land and Freedom Army and the resistance movement to British repression. The Mau Mau was primarily a rural terrorist group but it also began to develop support in urban areas where post-war living standards had declined as unemployment had risen.

Kikuyu tradition demanded the swearing of oaths. The oath became part of an initiation ceremony that irrevocably committed the member to fight to overthrow white rule and white culture in Kenya. The oath quickly became a 'killing oath'. Mau Mau methods included the murder and mutilation of so-called native 'collaborators', cattle maiming and the murder of white settlers.

Jomo Kenyatta (left) with the Mau Mau leader 'Field Marshal' Kwariana

KEY PEOPLE

Jomo Kenyatta (c.1891–1978) Kenyatta was a leading Kenyan nationalist politician and a member of the Kikuyu tribe. In the 1930s he attended socialist meetings in London and later visited Russia. In his book *Facing Mount Kenya* (1938) he detailed his thoughts. He emphasised the importance of recognising indigenous culture as valid rather than the 'civilising' effect of modern capitalism. Basically, he rejected the Europeanising effect of colonialism. From 1947, he led the Kenyan African Union, which later became KANU. Once independence had been achieved, Kenyatta became the first President of Kenya and remained so until his death.

The Kikuyu A very large tribal group in Kenya. The vast majority of the members of Mau Mau were drawn from this tribe.

The round-up of suspected Mau Mau terrorists in Kenya

Although Kenyatta was never conclusively linked to the Mau Mau, he was arrested in 1952 and imprisoned until 1961.

The British response was to declare a state of emergency. Mass arrests of Kikuyu tribesmen were carried out and the suspects held in special detention camps. British security forces cleared the forests of Kikuyu to prevent them exploiting hiding places.

With the apparent defeat of Mau Mau terrorism by 1956, most white settlers now assumed that everything would revert to 'normal'. White control would be restored and there would be no possibility of Britain considering any moves towards Kenyan independence either completely, through membership of some form of central African federation including other African states, or indeed anything that could result in black African majority rule.

This was far from the reality that emerged between 1956 and 1963. Moves were made to establish a new constitution that offered wider enfranchisement to native Africans and equal representation for them on the new **Legislative Council** by 1957. The British also legalised political parties in Kenya, and in 1960 held the Lancaster House Conference to consider further constitutional changes. This conference accepted that Africans must have a majority in the legislature. In 1962, a second Lancaster House Conference was called and this formally agreed to Kenyan independence from December 1963. On 12 December 1963.

Did the British accept independence for Kenya because of Mau Mau terrorism?

A review of the internal and external factors might shed some light on this issue.

- Mau Mau terrorism generated huge economic costs for Britain. It was estimated that to capture just one of the thousands of Mau Mau terrorists cost the British taxpayer about £10,000. Thus the financial cost of containing the terror was exorbitant. One of Macmillan's great priorities was to establish the real cost of colonial commitment and it was relatively easy for him to see this in Kenya.

- Despite this, there was the view that the Mau Mau was not a purely nationalist organisation. It was very much a Kikuyu peasant farmer group that aimed, primarily, to restore Kikuyu control in the White Highlands. It was not seen as being representative of the range of Kenyan thinking in terms of the struggle for independence. It was significant that far more black Kenyans than white settlers were killed during the terror.

- Throughout the 1950s, it gradually became clear that Kenyan nationalism could not be appeased. Any form of constitution that did not allow for black majority rule was doomed to fail. But the demands of the white settlers meant a continuance of white minority rule. Gradually, the constitutional reforms that were introduced led inexorably towards black majority rule.

- The process of independence was already underway in other east African states and Kenya became part of this momentum towards decolonisation. In 1961, Tanganyika (Tanzania) gained independence from Britain, as did Uganda in 1963.

- In 1960, when Macmillan's new Colonial Secretary announced constitutional change, the Governor, Sir Patrick Renison, declared that Kenyatta would never be released from prison. This provoked a whole new outburst of oath taking, which suggested a scale of internal chaos such as existed in the newly independent **Congo**. The Mau Mau's influence was clearly still potent and Britain was not willing to ignore it.

- Political developments after the neutralisation of Mau Mau were highly significant in gaining independence for Kenya. New political leaders emerged, most notably **Oginga Odinga** and **Tom Mboya**. They were able to create a new intertribal movement rather than the narrow Mau Mau–Kikuyu tribe focus. These men marked the start of a post-colonial political awareness

KEY EVENT

The Congo, 1960 In 1960, Belgium effectively abandoned its colony in central Africa. Almost immediately a civil war fought between rival tribal groups erupted. The chaos and the slaughter were only ended by the intervention of the United Nations.

KEY PEOPLE

Oginga Odinga (1924-94) He was associated with the campaign for Kenyan independence since the 1940s and was close to Kenyatta. Between 1952 and 1957 he was President of the Luo Union, a political and social organisation. In 1957 he was elected onto the Legislative Council and in 1960 he became vice president of KANU, the Kenyan African National Union. From 1966 he split with Kenyatta and was finally expelled from KANU in 1981.

Tom Mboya (1930-69) He was a Kenyan politician who founded the Kenyan African National Union (KANU). From 1964, once Kenya had gained its independence, he was Minister for Economic Affairs. In 1969 he was assassinated.

that convinced Britain that Kenya was politically mature enough for independence. In addition, the New Kenyan Group was formed by 1960. This was a group of white businessmen who wanted a negotiated settlement with African politicians in order to protect their business interests in Kenya. The white settler farming community began to leave the White Highlands as their power and land values declined.

Kenyan independence was the outcome of a new international context. Britain could no longer afford to be an imperial power and it no longer needed to be one. The Mau Mau made a contribution to independence but its significance should in no way be exaggerated.

THE WIND OF CHANGE: DECOLONISATION DECLARED?

In February 1960, the British Prime Minister, **Harold Macmillan**, addressed the South African Parliament. This followed recent visits to Ghana, Nigeria, and the Federation of Rhodesia and Nyasaland. Macmillan's speech graphically illustrated his thinking on Britain's African colonies and the issue of decolonisation:

In the twentieth century, and especially since the end of the war, we have seen the awakening of national consciousness in people who have for centuries lived in dependence on some other power.

He went on to say:

The wind of change is blowing through this continent, and, whether we like it or not, this growth of national consciousness is a political fact. We must all accept it as a fact, and our national policies must take account of it.

What significance did Macmillan's 'wind of change' speech have in explaining Britain's decolonisation policy?

- Macmillan assumed office after Eden's disaster at Suez. The nature of the defeat at Suez was evident to all Africans. The weaknesses of their colonial master had become patently clear to Africans struggling to achieve their own independence. This reality was not lost on Macmillan. Suez had shown, once and for all, that the battle for imperial prestige had been fought and lost.

- Although he did not explicitly state it, Macmillan was moved by economic factors. One of the first decisions he made concerning colonial policy was to commission a review of the costs of the empire compared to the gains it offered to Britain. The outcome of this review showed that British investments in non-colonial markets were more profitable than in colonial ones. Britain was no longer benefiting economically from its empire and any withdrawal from colonialism would have no economic cost to Britain. If anything, colonial investment was undermining investment in Britain. There was no longer a positive economic reason for maintaining formal control.

- This inevitably shaped political priorities for Macmillan. In the 1959 Budget, the Conservatives aimed to stimulate employment and prosperity through tax cuts and wage increases. One of Macmillan's political priorities was to strengthen Conservatism in Britain through economic development. By reducing Britain's colonial commitments, Macmillan reduced costs and reinforced the Conservative Party's political popularity.

- To reinforce this political objective, the Conservatives also realised that Britain could exploit more lucrative trade markets in the USA and Europe rather than colonial markets. Although initially reluctant to join the EEC in 1957, by 1961 Macmillan made a significant redirection in political and economic policy by seeking to join the EEC and move from an imperial to a regional, pro-European, economic basis.

- The changing international situation was also an important factor in Macmillan's thinking. In 1958, De Gaulle, the French Premier, made the initial offer of independence to France's African Empire. This contributed to the creation of a very unstable position in Africa, and, as other European states decolonised, made Britain look like an old-fashioned colonial oppressor. This simply fuelled further nationalist pressure amongst some of Britain's remaining African colonies.

- Decolonisation in Africa was already underway. In 1956 Sudan had gained independence and in 1957 it was Ghana's turn, although Britain did experience some difficulties in withdrawing from the High Commission territories in southern Africa because of concerns that they may fall under South African control.

It is important to note that a central element in Britain's decolonisation strategy was to replace formal empire with informal influence, based on favourable economic and defence treaties. Britain had to be seen to be cooperating to ensure that post-colonial relations were favourable to its economic and strategic needs.

In essence, Macmillan was a practical man whose priority was to protect and promote Britain's economic and strategic future in a new post-1945 world order. An imperial presence in Africa was increasingly less relevant to the achievement of these objectives.

WHAT WERE THE PROBLEMS FACING BRITAIN IN DECOLONISING MALAYA AND HONG KONG?

Malaya

This territory had been under British rule since 1826. Malaya was an unusually complex colony in that it was made up of a dozen states. Some of the component states, such as Singapore, were crown colonies and were ruled directly from London. Others, like the Malay States, were ruled by local Sultans who collaborated with British Commissioners. The population was ethnically complex. In addition to the native Malays, there was an equal number of Chinese, but also a smaller group of ethnic Indians and some white Europeans.

The above factors all contributed to Britain's reluctance to move towards decolonisation. A key issue in British decolonisation was the importance of retaining positive relations with the former colony. The complex nature of Malaya threatened this British objective. Malaya had vital raw materials, such as tin and rubber, which earned money Britain could use to pay off its war debts. Economically, Malaya was valuable to Britain. Singapore was regarded as a vital strategic area in the Far East. Britain was keen to maintain its positive strategic and economic interests '**East of Suez**'.

The anti-British violence in Malaya, known as the **Malayan Emergency**, was not the result of aggressive nationalism or terrorism but of ideological opposition. In 1948, Malaya had been established as a federation of states with a central government in overall control. This was dominated by the largest ethnic group, the Malays. In protest, many ethnic Chinese formed communist guerrilla groups. The Cold War context meant Britain would strongly oppose any decolonisation that might let in pro-communist influence. In June 1948, **martial law** was declared. The Malays supported British rule because Britain had promised independence as soon as the country was ready for it and because the communist terrorists were Chinese.

By 1953, middle-class Chinese had formed the Malayan Chinese Association while the Indian community had the Malayan Indian Congress. These two groups were both anti-communist and formed the Alliance Party with the United Malays' National Organisation. In effect, the communist threat had generated ethnic unity amongst the Malayan ruling classes. This stability persuaded the British to admit Malaya to the Commonwealth in 1957. Britain retained some influence and strategic advantage by agreeing to assist with internal and external security. Malaya was also to remain within the sterling area.

Tunku Abdul Rahman became the new leader of Malaya. In 1961, Malaya accepted the inclusion of Borneo, Sarawak, Brunei and Singapore in order to form the Federation of Malaysia, which formally came into being in September 1963.

Essentially, the pace of decolonisation in Malaya was the result of ethnic complications and a determination to prevent the spread of communism in South East Asia. Unlike in many African colonies, decolonisation was not the product of the efforts of nationalist movements. In 1963 Britain withdrew from North Borneo to facilitate the creation of Malaysia.

Hong Kong

The decolonisation of Hong Kong was unlike any previous British decolonisation. This was largely because the background to Hong Kong's existence as a British colony was also radically different from most of the rest of the British Empire.

- The island of Hong Kong had been acquired in 1842 as a result of **the Opium War**. Under the terms of the

KEY TERM

Martial law This is normally declared during a period of extreme crisis and disorder. In effect, the authority of a state's civil and criminal laws is removed and the military exercises the rule of law. For example, those suspected of crimes may be arrested by the military and tried and punished by them.

KEY PERSON

Tunku Abdul Rahman (1903–90) He was a Malaysian politician who became Prime Minister of the newly independent Malaya in 1957 until 1963. Between 1963 and 1970 he was Prime Minister of the collection of States which became Malaysia.

KEY EVENT

The Opium War, 1839–42 A war between Britain and China. Britain wanted to ensure that China imported opium, a lucrative trade. The Treaty of Nanking ended the war and forced China to accept free trade, including trade in opium. A number of Chinese ports were opened to Britain, including Canton and Shanghai.

Treaty of Nanking (1842), Britain had agreed to return the island by 1997. The mainland part of the colony had been leased from China in 1898.

- From 1949, Hong Kong's colonial existence had been dependent upon the tolerance of the newly created communist China.
- Because of this context, Britain had done very little to prepare for the self-government of Hong Kong. Instead, Hong Kong had developed as a leading commercial and banking centre in the Far East. Part of the logic in this approach was to make Hong Kong a valuable asset, which China would not damage when its control was finally restored. Also, Britain reasoned that while the colony prospered under British rule, it would be untroubled. This economic structure was to be maintained for 50 years under a Sino–British agreement made in 1984. Some very limited representative government had been introduced by 1984 and the intention was that this move towards some democracy would also be preserved under Chinese rule.

For Britain, the decolonisation process was a legal requirement under the terms of earlier agreements. The emphasis had to be on protecting Hong Kong's post-colonial future when faced with a takeover by a communist state. This became particularly important after China's response to the pro-democracy movement and the events of **Tiananmen Square** in 1989. This was a unique scenario in British decolonisation. In 1992, the new Governor of Hong Kong, Chris Patten, advanced the process of democratisation despite China's protests.

The decolonisation of Hong Kong was the final act in Britain's disengagement from empire and it was characterised by the classic imperialist argument of carrying out a duty towards the people of the colony.

SUMMARY QUESTIONS

1. Explain why Britain withdrew from India in 1947.

2. To what extent was the Suez Crisis a turning point in decolonisation?

3. Assess the importance of any three major reasons that influenced Britain's decision to decolonise after 1945.

CHAPTER 9

How and why did Britain contribute to the Cold War up to 1953?

In the aftermath of the Second World War, Britain's foreign policy priorities centred around the belief expressed by the Foreign Secretary, **Ernest Bevin**, when he insisted that 'we regard ourselves as one of the powers most vital to the peace of the world'. Britain did not see its role in international relations as that of a second-rate power clinging to the coat-tails of its protector, the USA. However, Britain did regard the USA as its most important ally and therefore became closely linked to US foreign policy thinking. This was particularly true in terms of Anglo–American relations with the Soviet Union. Ideologically, economically and strategically, Britain's interests were closely linked to those of the USA. This inevitably meant that as **the Cold War** developed, Britain's contribution was strongly supportive of US objectives. However, though Britain believed it could maintain a superpower status; the reality was that it was dependent upon the patronage of the USA, the country that did have the necessary economic, military and strategic power.

THE DESCENT OF THE IRON CURTAIN?

Britain and the Soviet Union

After the 1945 general election, the Labour Party formed the government. Attlee's Foreign Secretary was Ernest Bevin. Although both were socialists, neither regarded the Soviet Union as a natural ally of Britain. Indeed, both had fought to keep communist influence out of the Labour Party.

In February 1945, at the Yalta Conference, the Allies had agreed to the Declaration on Liberated Europe. This committed them, amongst other things, to:

form interim governmental authorities broadly representative of all democratic elements in the population and pledged to the earliest possible establishment through free elections of governments responsive to the will of the people.

KEY PERSON

Ernest Bevin (1881–1951)
Bevin was a Labour politician and a leading British trade unionist. In 1921, he founded the Transport and General Workers' Union and remained its General Secretary until he joined Churchill's wartime coalition Cabinet in 1940 as Minister of Labour and National Service. Bevin was a socialist and supreme defender of the interests of the British working class but he was not a communist. In 1945, he became Foreign Secretary and remained in that post until his death in 1951.

KEY EVENT

The Cold War, 1945-90
The term Cold War describes the ideological, political and economic tensions that existed between the USA and its western allies on one side and the USSR and its communist allies on the other. The relationship between the two sides was based on profound distrust and led, during the 1950s, to a nuclear arms race. By the late 1980s the Soviet Union's influence in Eastern Europe had declined and there was a willingness to move towards arms reduction agreements. The Cold War officially ended in 1990.

Stalin, however, was merely giving lip service to this agreement. In reality, the Soviet Union was working towards the destruction of democracy in Eastern Europe and the creation of pro-Soviet communist governments. This process certainly appeared to be underway in Poland, Bulgaria and Romania. The creation of Eastern European states friendly towards the Soviet Union was acceptable to Britain provided that democracy, and therefore a multiparty political system, prevailed. The decline in Anglo–Soviet relations was centred on the following issues:

- In July 1945, a communist government backed by the Soviet Union was installed in Poland.
- Communism as an ideology was strong in Italy and France and there was the real possibility that it would spread throughout the rest of the devastated states of post-war Europe.
- The Soviet Foreign Minister, Molotov, stated that the Soviet Union had the absolute right to determine the political structure of post-war Eastern Europe.
- Reports from British representatives in Moscow suggested that there was 'hardly any doubt any longer that the Soviet Union is intent on the destruction of the British Empire'. Britain was convinced that it faced aggressive communism. There was the belief that communism sought to spread, particularly by taking advantage of the social and economic chaos caused by the Second World War. The notion of worldwide communism was particularly prevalent in the British Foreign Office at the time.

The Soviet interpretation of its 'apparent' expansionism in Eastern Europe was based on the need to establish firm security against future aggression. Winston Churchill's speech in March 1946 placed a completely different spin on Soviet actions.

The speech
There was a profound gap between the Soviet view of events and those of Britain. Stalin said in a speech made in March 1946:

The Germans made their invasion of the USSR through Finland, Poland and Rumania. They were able to invade because these countries were hostile to the Soviet Union. What is surprising about the fact that the Soviet Union, anxious for its own security, is trying to see to it that governments loyal in their attitudes to the Soviet Union should exist in Eastern Europe?

Churchill's perception of events in Eastern Europe was vastly different and he made this clear in a speech he delivered on 5 March 1946 in Fulton Missouri, USA.

A cartoon entitled 'A peep under the Iron Curtain' published in 1946

From Stettin in the Baltic, to Trieste in the Adriatic, an iron curtain has descended. Behind that line lie the capitals of the states of Central and Eastern Europe. All these cities lie in the Soviet sphere and all are subject to a very high and increasing measure of control from Moscow. In many countries throughout the world, communist groups are established and work in absolute obedience to directions they receive from the communist centre, Moscow.

Churchill's speech was not a dispassionate and objective analysis of the reality of Soviet actions in Eastern Europe and the motives underlying them.

Why did Churchill make such a speech and what contribution did it make to the development of the Cold War?

The primary motive was consistent with that of British government policy. Britain needed to draw the USA into some form of security alliance in order to protect Western Europe. Churchill contributed to the **demonisation of the Soviet Union** and his speech was delivered in the heart of anti-communist USA at a time when US sensitivities towards Soviet actions in Eastern Europe were at their height. How could the USA ignore such a prophetic message as that implied in Churchill's speech? Only by adding to US fears of the threat posed by communism could Churchill push the USA into a more defined and firmer anti-Soviet policy, which would ultimately benefit Britain and the rest of Western Europe.

How did the Truman Doctrine and the Marshall Plan escalate the Cold War?

The speech was merely one element amongst many that drove US foreign policy thinking but it did make a major contribution to Truman's decision to adopt a policy of **containment**. This was expressed through what became known as **the Truman Doctrine**.

MARSHALL AID

Britain had been funding the military costs of the Greek government's campaign to prevent Greek communists from seizing the country. In February 1947, Britain announced that it could no longer continue its aid to Greece. This was a vital factor in pushing the USA into offering financial aid designed to stop the spread of communism and bolster the Truman Doctrine and containment.

For Britain, the crucial factor in the **Marshall Plan** was that it offered economic aid to Western Germany. The Plan also guaranteed strategic and political influence for the USA in Western Europe. This was, it was believed, the ideal method to stem the spread of communism and thereby compliment containment. The USSR responded to the Marshall Plan by setting up Cominform, an organisation to coordinate the activities of the Communist parties in Bulgaria, Hungary, Czechoslovakia, France, Italy, Poland, Romania, the USSR and Yugoslavia.

Bevin played a major role in coordinating a Western European response to the USA's economic aid package. In January 1947, Britain had already agreed to merge its zone in Germany with the US zone. Britain's strategy in this and its support for the Marshall Plan was a major contributory factor to the division of Germany. As the western sectors flourished economically, it was clear to the Soviets that Western Germany was being prepared for post-war reunification. In June 1948, a new currency was introduced into the western sector. The Soviets immediately blockaded West Berlin. **The Berlin blockade** was the final step towards the division of Germany.

Britain's policies did not cause the Cold War to develop. It was the USA who was the prime mover in international relations and it was the USA who had most to gain by creating a Cold War relationship with the Soviet Union. By generating a climate of fear in Europe the USA could then present itself as Europe's protector. However, Britain did encourage such a policy and certainly saw itself as a superpower that would also benefit from US policy in

Europe towards the Soviet Union. Britain contributed to the crisis to which the USA chose to react. The USSR was not entirely without blame for the development of the Cold War, particularly as it established communist regimes throughout Easten Europe. By 1949, Germany was divided and the USA was committed to protecting Western Europe.

HOW DID STRATEGIC ISSUES CONTRIBUTE TO THE COLD WAR?

Nuclear weapons

In January 1947, Britain formally decided to develop its own nuclear capability. This decision was not simply a way of attempting to present Britain as a global power, although it was clear that nuclear weapons were an essential prerequisite of superpower status. It was part of a calculated response to the perceived Soviet threat. Unlike the USA, Britain lay within easy striking distance of Soviet bombers, which could deliver a nuclear attack.

Nuclear explosion at Hiroshima, 1945

In August 1946, the USA ended its collaboration with Britain on the research and development of nuclear technology. Partly as a result of this, Britain was not convinced that the USA could be fully relied upon to defend Western Europe in the event of a communist attack. In August 1949, the Soviet Union successfully tested its nuclear technology and this increased pressure on Britain to develop its nuclear capability. Finally, in October 1952, Britain successfully tested its own atomic bomb on the Monte Bello islands in the Pacific Ocean.

Britain's ability to develop its own nuclear capability was essential. This development did not accelerate the Cold War. As both sides held nuclear power, that power created a balance and the balance maintained peace. East–West relations may have been frosty but it was believed that they would never degenerate into global conflict with weapons of mass destruction. Nuclear technology created stability rather than instability in international relations. It was the supreme deterrent.

THE FORMATION OF NATO: AN OFFENSIVE OR DEFENSIVE ALLIANCE?

Background

The significant and immediate events preceding the creation of NATO were **the communist coup in Czechoslovakia** (February 1948) and the Berlin Blockade (June 1948–May 1949). The first steps towards closer cooperation in Western Europe had been taken in March 1948 when Britain, France, Belgium, Holland and Luxembourg signed **the Brussels Defence Treaty**. This committed the member states to military cooperation in time of war and marked the beginnings of an attempt to develop a common defence system and to strengthen military ties between the members. On 4 March 1949, this was extended through the North Atlantic Treaty signed in Washington. The USA, Canada, Denmark, Iceland, Portugal, Italy and Norway joined the Brussels alliance members. This treaty created NATO.

What role did Britain play in the formation of NATO and what significance did this have in the development of the Cold War?

Superficially, it might appear that the USA was determined to establish a stronger presence in Europe and thereby a regional superpower presence through gathering Western European states together under its leadership in an act of **collective security** in order to make the US policy of containment a reality. This suggests that the USA provided the impetus for the creation of NATO. Such a view would also suggest that Britain's role was merely that of a passive follower of US Cold War policy, rather than a driving influence on US policy. This view profoundly distorts the role Britain played in the creation of NATO and, therefore, minimises the contribution Britain made to the development of the Cold War up to 1953. What other factors need to be considered in order to establish a clearer understanding of Britain's role in terms of NATO?

- NATO represented the cornerstone of British foreign policy by 1949. Ernest Bevin, the British Foreign Secretary, contributed significantly towards the shaping of US initiatives which culminated in NATO. By early 1948, Bevin was convinced that a divided Europe was unavoidable. The Soviet veto on Marshall Aid for Eastern Europe and the communist seizure of power in Czechoslovakia in February 1948 convinced Bevin that the partition of Europe was gaining momentum. The logic of this pointed to an ever-growing threat from the Soviet Union. In January 1948, Prime Minister Attlee commented that 'Soviet communism pursues a policy of imperialism in a new form – ideological, economic and strategic – which threatens the welfare and way of life of the other nations of Europe.' A firm alliance system had to be established in order to protect Western Europe from the threat of communist ideological, economic and military aggression.

- By 1948, Bevin's objectives were twofold.

  1 He called for a 'Western Union', which sought to establish closer cooperation between the states of Western Europe.

  2 He regarded the USA as a world power that had the wealth and the political commitment to support Western Europe.

  The USA needed to be convinced that Europe was willing to offer some of its own resources to help itself and that there would not simply be wholesale unconditional support from the USA. Bevin was the driving force behind the Brussels Defence Treaty. He knew that this would be enough to lure the USA into defending Western Europe.

- Bevin's strategy was strengthened when, in June 1948, the Russians blockaded Berlin. He was able to promote the idea of an airlift. The joint Anglo–American airlift enabled Berlin to survive for the eleven months of the blockade. The crisis catapulted the Brussels Defence Treaty into its new form – NATO. Bevin had skilfully structured British policy to ensure that Britain was able to exploit the situation in Europe between 1948 and 1949 and draw the USA into a powerful regional defence alliance.

Britain's influence in bringing the USA into NATO should not be overstated. There was undoubtedly a conviction within the US government that such a regional alliance was

The Korean War, 1950-3
North Korean communist forces invaded South Korea. The USA, under the UN flag, sent troops to defend the south from this threat. Britain also entered this war. The war heightened the anxiety that Western European leaders felt about the threat from communism and the vulnerability of their own states.

The Warsaw Pact, 1955
Otherwise known as the Eastern European Mutual Assistance Pact. This was a military agreement between Eastern European communist states and the Soviet Union. It was designed to establish a united military defence system against any external threats from the Western European capitalist states. It was originally set up as a response to the admission of West Germany into NATO.

also in its national interests. It was the logical next step in the realisation of containment. In addition, Article 5 of the Brussels Defence Treaty enabled the USA to choose whether it would use military force or not. Until the outbreak of the **Korean War** in 1950, the NATO alliance was not a tight-knit defence alliance. This was made graphically clear by the words of a US politician, Averell Harriman, when he commented that it took the Korean War to 'put the "O" in NATO'.

The USA's commitment to NATO had some very significant advantages for Britain.

- Criticism against defence spending reduced as more people became convinced of the Soviet threat.
- Britain's defence spending was being subsidised by US spending.
- Despite its increasing reliance upon the USA, Britain was not faced with the prime responsibility of European defence and could therefore develop its global role as a potential world power more fully. Britain still retained aspirations of world power status and NATO was seen as a contributory factor in enabling this to develop. Britain's policy was founded on exploiting US power in order to enhance its own international status.

The creation of NATO had a significant impact on the development of the Cold War. It convinced Stalin of the need to consolidate Soviet control of Eastern Europe and to develop the communist version of NATO. Thus emerged the **Warsaw Pact** in 1955.

WHAT WAS THE SIGNIFICANCE OF THE KOREAN WAR (1950–3) ON THE DEVELOPMENT OF THE COLD WAR?

Although Anglo–American relations appeared to be harmonious in March 1949, their relationship was under pressure by October of that year. Britain knew that the US fear of communism and the adoption of containment had worked to its own advantage in Western Europe. However, containment had also deepened the breakdown of East–West relations and this could create new problems beyond Europe in which Britain may have to be involved through its commitment to the USA. This was exactly the position in which Britain found itself by 1950.

Did Britain's policy towards the Korean War make a significant contribution to the expansion of the Cold War?

The problem of communist expansionism, which containment was designed to prevent, first erupted beyond Europe in the Far East. In October 1949, China was declared a communist state after their victory in the civil war. The USA refused to recognise the new regime and the assumption was that their close ally, Britain, would do the same. Bevin and the Foreign Office disagreed. Britain's interests would be best served by recognising China's new regime because:

- the British colony of Hong Kong was very vulnerable to Chinese aggression
- British commercial interests in China were significant and non-recognition would damage these
- the most effective way to minimise Soviet influence in China would be for the West to recognise the regime there. This would weaken international communist unity and therefore communist expansionism elsewhere in the world.

In January 1950, Britain recognised the official existence of communist China. In June 1950, forces from communist North Korea crossed the **38th Parallel** and invaded non-communist South Korea.

What was British policy in the Korean War?

Inevitably, British policy was designed to protect British interests.

- Britain was a firm ally of the USA and as such offered support when the USA initiated UN action to be taken against North Korea in order to protect the South. Britain also committed 10,000 troops.
- On the other hand, Britain was concerned that this Asian conflict should not divert US support away from Europe, a key element of Britain's relationship with the USA. Containment was becoming globalised and this was certainly not a direction Britain wanted to move in.
- US talk of using nuclear weapons provoked an immediate British reaction. Attlee visited Washington in December 1950 to ensure that such a course of action was prevented. He did not succeed in securing a

KEY TERM

38th Parallel With the defeat of its Japanese occupiers in 1945, Korea was divided along the 38th parallel. This was to be temporary and it was the result of Soviet troops liberating the north and US troops liberating the south. In 1948 a communist government was set up in the north and a non-communist one in the south. In 1949 US and Soviet troops withdrew from Korea.

commitment from the Americans that atomic weapons would categorically not be used. Any such commitment would have undermined the whole idea of nuclear weapons acting as a deterrent.

An immediate consequence of the war for Britain was that the defence budget rose from £2.3 billion in 1950 to £4.7 billion in 1951. Although Britain did have options in the Korean War, it was fundamentally committed to backing US policy. A determination to preserve the security of Europe through US support meant Britain contributed towards the expansion of the Cold War, albeit reluctantly. Britain did not have the power to function as an equal partner with the USA and therefore became complicit in the USA's deepening of the Cold War but made only a limited contribution of its own towards this process. The USA was able to demand that Britain increase its defence spending and Britain was not in a position to reject this demand. This illustrates Britain's second-rate status as a world power, despite the view of the British Ambassador in Washington that Britain was, by 1950, 'one of the two world powers outside Russia'.

Britain's contribution to the Cold War lay in its inability to defend itself and its inability to contribute significantly to the defence of Europe. Britain had to lure the USA and it was this US interventionism that led to the globalisation of East–West confrontation for the next 45 years.

SUMMARY QUESTIONS

1   Why did Britain regard the USA as crucial to the defence of Europe between 1945 and 1953? Explain your answer.

2   Explain why NATO was created in 1949.

3   Assess the importance of Britain's contribution to the development of the Cold War between 1945 and 1953.

CHAPTER 10

Why did Britain reject European integration in 1957, but then apply to join the EEC four years later?

BRITAIN AND EUROPEAN UNION, 1945–57

It was in 1957 that Britain formally refused to join a new united Europe when it did not sign up to the Treaty of Rome. The key issue at this point is how and why did a united Europe emerge and why had Britain adopted the stance it took before 1957?

Beginnings

In the immediate post-war years there were a range of reasons why a more united Europe was seen as desirable:

- integration would mean war was far less likely to happen again
- in a bi-polar world, Western European states could not compete with the USA or the USSR unless they united as a regional group
- economic reconstruction would be easier
- economic integration would also promote large scale, low cost production and favourable intrastate trade opportunities
- in the face of communist expansionism, unity would reinforce Western Europe's strategic and ideological strength
- the USA favoured closer cooperation amongst European states because this would enaable Western Europe to better defend itself, rather than adopting a total dependency approach towards the USA.

The fundamental British attitude towards being part of any form of European union had been summed up by Winston Churchill before the war and this view was shared by the post-war Labour government. Churchill had said:

We are with Europe but not of it. We are linked but not compromised. We are interested and associated but not absorbed.

The Organisation for European Economic Cooperation (OEEC), 1948

The USA provided economic aid through the Marshall Plan. Seventeen European nations set up the OEEC to distribute the funds and promote trade. Rather than being a major step towards European unification, the OEEC was an international and not a **supranational** organisation. The OEEC was consistent with British thinking on European economic issues. It did not represent an integrated organisation and it did not move Europe closer towards any form of economic union or a **customs union**.

Britain was committed to the belief that its economic interests lay with the Commonwealth and not a European economic union. Half of Britain's exports went to the sterling area while only a quarter went to Western Europe. In 1947, the combined exports of France, Germany, Italy, Norway and Denmark only equalled those of Britain. In essence, Britain's economic future lay in protecting the sterling area, not in joining a European customs union. France, therefore, took the creation of a European supranational body aimed at economic integration.

Was the Schuman Plan of 1950 the first step towards European unity?

In May 1950, the French Foreign Minister, **Robert Schuman,** launched an idea that had originally been proposed by a French economist, Jean Monnet. Schuman's Plan was that the coal and steel resources of France and Germany should be combined and administered by a supranational authority. Eventually all tariffs in these heavy industries were to be removed. The primary objective was to ensure France's security by preventing Germany having total control of the industries that had been at the heart of its war effort. But the Plan was about much more than simply the preservation of French security in the face of a newly created West German federal state. It also represented the first major step in a programme that would, sector by sector, remove national economic barriers in Europe. In 1952, Schuman's proposals came to fruition when France, Germany, Belgium, Holland, Luxembourg and Italy ('the Six') agreed to set up the European Coal and Steel Community (ECSC). Britain became an associate member of the ECSC in December 1954 but, significantly, had refused to join the six in 1952.

- The British coal industry had just been nationalised. Britain's coal and steel industries were strong and determined to protect their global markets. Only five per cent of British steel went to Western Europe.
- The Plan was seen as a French device to protect its security against a possible German threat.
- Britain could not accept the supranational character of the Plan. The issue of British **national sovereignty** was central to this approach. Cooperation with Europe did not mean surrendering Britain's sovereignty, as the Schuman Plan demanded, it meant intergovernmental links with Britain retaining its overall power to make its own policy in its own national interests.
- A Foreign Office official revealed which of Britain's other interests would be at risk if they backed the Plan when he commented: 'We shall have tipped the balance against the other two elements in our world situation, the Atlantic community and the Commonwealth.'

KEY TERM

National sovereignty The ability of an independent state to govern its own affairs through its own institutions without submitting any authority to another institution over which it has no absolute control.

How did Britain respond to the Treaty of Rome?

Messina, 1955

The Foreign Ministers of the Six met in Messina, Sicily, to begin 'a fresh advance towards the building of Europe'. Primarily, the aim was to establish a customs union that would lead to a European common market. Britain was invited to join the discussions and responded by sending a Board of Trade Official, Russell Bretherton, to act as their representative 'without commitment'. Britain displayed a clear disregard for the opportunity it had at the Messina talks to have a leading role in the creation of a united Europe. There was a degree of consistency in Britain's reasoning for not joining with the Six.

- The importance of Britain's non-European economic interests were more central to Britain's economic future than any opportunities in Western Europe. The economic opportunities through the empire and the Commonwealth outweighed the drive towards economic integration in Europe.
- Membership of a protectionist European common market could undermine its global trade as existing trading partners rejected Britain's protectionist commitment to Europe and took their business elsewhere.

- Economic union was seen as a major step towards the longer-term scenario of political union. Britain was not prepared to submit its national sovereignty to a Western European federalist system. This, the British government believed, was the logical progression of developments from Messina.

- Britain's economy was strong but not the strongest in Europe. In addition, Britain was the only nuclear power besides the USA and the USSR. Why should Britain join what amounted to a collection of second-rate Western European powers?

The Treaty of Rome, 1957

Member states in 1957

EEC membership by 1957

In March 1957, the Treaty of Rome was signed by the Six and on 1 January 1958, the European Economic Community (EEC) came into existence. Britain's actions up to and following the signing of the Treaty of Rome are particularly revealing in terms of its attitudes towards European union. Britain's priorities were to:

Why did Britain reject European integration in 1957, but then apply to join the EEC four years later?

- safeguard its relations with the USA. Britain feared that the EEC would become an increasingly powerful economic and political force in Europe and thereby capable of exercising considerable international influence. The British government noted:

Our special relationship with the USA would be endangered if the US believed that our influence was less than that of the European Community.

- safeguard its relations with the Commonwealth. Britain proposed a European free trade area for industrial goods but not agriculture. Members of this proposed area could negotiate their own import tariff levels with non-members and they would not be limited by common external tariff rates of the kind the EEC was applying. This would have the effect of protecting Commonwealth agricultural interests and thereby maintain and strengthen the important economic and political links Britain had with the Commonwealth. The foundation of these links were established at **the Ottawa Conference** of 1932.

In its own political and economic interests, Britain had to be involved in Europe. Britain's strategy was based on association with, but not membership of, the European Economic Community. This was very consistent with what had preceded the Treaty of Rome. The economic aim was to take advantage of the free trade opportunities in European markets while retaining close trading links with the Commonwealth. The political aim was to ensure that non-membership of the EEC did not lead to Britain's isolation. Britain could not afford, politically, to allow a stronger, united Europe to overshadow its relationship with the USA. Britain wanted to retain the Atlantic alliance because it was an integral part of its strategic defence plan.

Britain's determination was so great that Macmillan even voiced threats such as:

if 'Little Europe' is formed without a parallel development of a free trade area, we shall have to reconsider the whole of our political and economic attitudes towards Europe...I doubt if we could remain in NATO...We should take our troops out of Europe.

KEY AGREEMENT

The Ottawa Conference, 1932 Britain abandoned free trade and established agreements based upon imperial preference. This enabled Commonwealth states to protect themselves from foreign competition by applying high tariffs.

These threats had no effect. In December 1958, France refused to accept Britain's plans and the other five EEC members supported this opposition. This French initiative raised another factor in understanding Britain's attitude towards Europe at this time.

The French President, **Charles de Gaulle**, was convinced that Britain was a serious rival to France becoming the dominant influence in Europe. Macmillan's threat clearly illustrated that Britain saw itself as the dominant influence and was pushing its own plans forward in order to guarantee that influence. Britain, since 1945, had not been content to act as a second-rate power. It needed influence in Europe, and the creation of the EEC was seen as a challenge to this and to Britain's global power. If the Six would not join a free trade association then other European states might. Britain continued to pursue this objective of a free trade association outside the EEC.

Why did Britain back the European Free Trade Association (EFTA) in 1959?

In November 1959, Britain, Denmark, Norway, Sweden, Austria, Switzerland and Portugal signed the Stockholm Convention and agreed to create the EFTA. This reinforced the belief among Europeans and the USA that Britain had ruled out the idea of joining the EEC. Why did Britain pursue this drive towards a free trade association and create this alternative organisation?

- The EFTA's economic aims were to work for tariff reductions. Britain saw this as a way of bringing the EEC Six into further talks that might lead to a multilateral trading agreement between the EFTA and the EEC members.
- It was a necessary alternative group that Britain hoped would enable it to influence Europe without compromising British national sovereignty.

BRITAIN AND THE EEC, 1961–3

Just two years after the formation of EFTA, the British government announced its intention to apply for admission into the EEC. The central player in this decision was Harold Macmillan.

KEY PERSON

Charles de Gaulle (1890–1970) Before he became a political leader, de Gaulle was a soldier. He served in the First World War. In 1940, he went into exile and organised the Free French Forces fighting the Germans. At the end of the war he became head of the provisional French government until he resigned in 1946. He formed his own Gaullist Party and became its leader. Between 1958 and 1969, he was President of France. He introduced a new presidential form of constitution in order to bring greater stability to French politics. He supported decolonisation in France's African empire and he wanted to strengthen France's power

Why had Britain's attitude towards the EEC apparently changed so radically?

- Britain still wanted to preserve a close relationship with the USA, the 'special relationship'. President Eisenhower had shown strong support for the EEC and his successor, Kennedy, wanted Britain to join the EEC in order to limit the ambitions of France in Europe. In April 1961, Kennedy made it perfectly clear to Macmillan that 'relations between the USA and the UK would be strengthened, not weakened, if the UK moved toward membership of the Six'. A Europe dominated by French influence would not be in the interests of either Britain or the USA. Kennedy wanted Europe to remain closely allied to, and partly dependent upon, the USA. The USA's vision of its relationship with Western Europe was based on interdependency. There would be a political, military and economic partnership, which would grow as the EEC became larger and more successful. Increased French influence might move Europe towards greater regional self-sufficiency and undermine the USA's influence. Britain was under pressure to prevent this by joining the EEC.
- The economic condition of the Six was steadily improving through the effects of the removal of the trade barriers between them. Economic growth in Britain was beginning to slow down.

Coal output

	Total UK output (millions of tons)	% exported
1950	216.3	6.2
1955	221.6	5.5
1960	193.6	2.6
1965	187.5	2.0

Macmillan's government was popular and he did not want to undermine that popularity by making unpopular decisions, such as reducing manning levels to improve Britain's industrial productivity. Entry into the EEC would offer Macmillan the opportunity to argue that competition from Europe led to, for example, reduced manning.

- The EFTA had not developed as a viable alternative to the EEC. Some EFTA members, including Britain, were trading more within the EEC than with their EFTA partners. The member states were not fully united in their attitudes towards the EEC. Denmark, for example, was keen to cooperate with the EEC and it was only its dependency upon the British market for agricultural products that restrained it. The EFTA appeared to offer few tangible benefits to its members compared to those offered by the EEC. Britain could not simply ignore this economic reality.

- The economic importance of the Commonwealth was diminishing. It became clear that trade with the Commonwealth faced a long-term steady decline. Between 1954 and 1960, Commonwealth trade with Britain increased by only one per cent. Britain's economic commitment to the Commonwealth was looking increasingly irrelevant. Commonwealth countries were expanding their own range of trading partners as their trade with Britain declined.

- A significant element of Macmillan's thinking lay in his determination to maintain Britain's influence as a world power. By 1960 the French were pushing for the development of the EEC as a political union. If Britain were not part of a regional political union in Western Europe, then this isolation might damage Britain's international status. Joining the EEC was necessary 'to preserve the power and strength of Britain in the world'.

What was the role of Macmillan?

Harold Macmillan began what many observers saw as a revolution in British policy. It seemed to be the beginning of a new commitment to Europe involving an abandonment of the 'special relationship' with the USA and the strong links Britain had developed with the Commonwealth. Macmillan wanted to preserve Britain's role as a world power and believed, finally, that this could best be achieved through membership of the EEC. Thus, Macmillan was remaining consistent with the primary post-war objectives of British policy.

Macmillan made some crucial decisions in order to prepare the ground for a British application to join the EEC. There were considerable divisions within his Cabinet. To neutralise these, Macmillan carried out a major Cabinet reshuffle in the summer of 1960. Christopher Soames went to Agriculture and Duncan Sandys to Commonwealth Relations. Both men were pro-European, as were Macmillan's other appointees. Edward Heath was made Lord Privy Seal and a Foreign Office minister. Heath became Britain's chief negotiator in 1961.

Britain's application was in no sense based on an unconditional acceptance of existing EEC arrangements and this was to prove a significant factor in its rejection. To this extent, Macmillan's responsibility for the failure had to be acknowledged. Macmillan's initial approach was not to commit Britain to joining but to find out if the terms for joining were acceptable to British interests. This immediately gave the impression that Macmillan was not a true pro-European and that Britain's entry would change the structure and character of the EEC. Britain wanted special arrangements to be made to cover Commonwealth trade, British agriculture and the EFTA.

"IF THEY WANT US THEY WILL HAVE TO MAKE IT EASY FOR US" —MR. MACMILLAN

British cartoon of Macmillan and De Gaulle published in 1963

Macmillan and the French

In January 1963, the French President, Charles de Gaulle, effectively vetoed Britain's entry. Was this the result of Macmillan's tactics or was there a French determination to prevent Britain's entry, which Macmillan could do nothing to prevent?

De Gaulle's attitude towards Britain was made very clear when he announced the French veto. He said:

England is, in effect, insular, maritime, linked through its trade, markets and food supply to very diverse and very distant countries…The question is to know if Great Britain can at present place itself with the Continent and like it, within a tariff that is truly common, give up all preference with regard to the Commonwealth, cease to claim that its agriculture be privileged, and even more, consider null and void the commitments it has made with the countries that are part of its free trade area.

In effect, de Gaulle doubted Britain's commitment to the Treaty of Rome, but there were other, possibly more significant factors that made Britain's entry almost impossible to achieve. Britain's entry could present a major challenge to French dominance in Europe and de Gaulle's own personal ambitions of European leadership. De Gaulle was vehemently opposed to any form of Atlantic partnership with the USA and he regarded Britain as a key factor in keeping US influence in Europe. The arrival of Polaris missiles into Britain from the USA reinforced de Gaulle's certainty that Britain was still profoundly committed to the Atlantic alliance with the USA.

In the face of these considerations, Macmillan's position was almost impossible. Even if Britain had presented itself as a committed pro-European state, de Gaulle would have rejected its entry. It was not Britain's links to the USA and the Commonwealth, and its obsession with national sovereignty, that defeated the application. Essentially, it was Gaullism. By 1958, de Gaulle was in place in France and the EEC was in existence. Britain would have been opposed in 1958. Despite this, Macmillan's tactics did not help. Britain wanted to enter the EEC for largely negative reasons. It feared that a developing EEC would undermine Britain's international role. Britain's actions were based on self-interest rather than a commitment to a developing European community.

Essentially, Macmillan had created an almost impossible task for himself. He wanted to strengthen Britain's ties with the USA and join Europe.

SUMMARY QUESTIONS

1   Explain why Britain refused to join the EEC in 1957.

2   Why did Britain's attitude to membership of the EEC change after 1957?

3   'The main reason for Britain's failure to gain membership of the EEC by 1963 was de Gaulle's opposition.' How far do you agree with this view?

AS ASSESSMENT

SOURCE BASED QUESTIONS IN THE STYLE OF AQA

This type of question would have 45 minutes allocated to it for your response and it would be one of two questions to be answered on a one-and-a-half hour paper. It is a useful technique in time management under examination conditions to use the mark allocation for each question part to determine roughly how long to spend on each answer. This should also give you an idea of how detailed you can allow your answers to get. A mark allocation of 3 out of 25, for example, would suggest that you should spend about five minutes on the answer.

Questions

Read the following source and then answer the questions that follow.

Bevin was convinced that a divided Europe was inevitable and it seemed essential to consolidate the western half or risk economic and political collapse, accelerated by the re-emergence of communist parties in Europe. From 1948, he pressed on the Americans the need for 'some form of union, formal or informal...in Western Europe, backed by the United States and the Dominions'.

Adapted from *Britannia Overruled*, D. Reynolds (1991)

Before answering these questions, you should read the relevant part of Chapter 7 and the whole of Chapter 9 in this book.

(a) Use the source and your own knowledge to comment on the term 'a divided Europe' in the context of British interests immediately after the end of the Second World War. (3 marks)

How to answer this question

- This question requires you to use the source **and** your own knowledge. If you only use one or the other, then the maximum mark you will achieve will be 1. Such an answer might suggest that Europe was divided after the war. The Western part was capitalist, while the Eastern half was communist. This would be a simple and underdeveloped factual statement.
- Although the question asks you to comment on the term in a particular context, to attain higher marks, it is necessary to **explain** the term in its context. This demonstrates understanding rather than merely knowledge. The source makes it clear that Britain recognised the reality of a permanently divided post-war Europe and the importance of the USA's role as a protector of Western Europe. The answer may then be developed to illustrate an understanding of British post-war foreign policy. Reference may be made to the importance Britain placed upon involving the USA in the defence of Europe and some explanation of why this was. Britain's economic problems could be highlighted here.

(b) Explain why Britain wanted to strengthen the protection of Western Europe.

(7 marks)

How to answer this question

- The answer to this question does not require direct reference to the source. Essentially there are three 'types' of response that are anticipated by examiners. The first may show some limited understanding through generalised and often unsupported statements. Such answers may simply suggest that Britain feared the spread of communism from Eastern Europe and needed help to stop it.

- The second 'type' of answer may demonstrate some understanding of one or two factors and use appropriate material to illustrate this. Answers may consider the British perception of the nature of the spread of communism, and particularly the spread of Soviet influence, in Eastern Europe by 1948. Britain certainly saw this as Soviet expansionism. Reference to the wider context may also reinforce this view. Soviet interest in the Middle East, Greece and Turkey may add weight to this view. Britain was in no position to maintain the security of Western Europe without some US support. Discusssion of Britain's economic and strategic limitations would reinforce this answer and offer a sound explanation of another factor.

- The third 'type' of response, and the one that certainly generates the highest reward, is that which demonstrates direct understanding of a range of factors and is able to make links between the factors, prioritise their relative importance, and draw valid conclusions. Such answers may well include references made in the previous paragraph but go on to emphasise that Britain's need to protect Western Europe was primarily linked to protecting British interests. An examination of Britain's foreign policy priorities is directly relevant here. Britain's aim was to develop both a European alliance and an Atlantic alliance as the foundation of long-term post-war security for Britain. Answers may well consider Britain's motives in promoting the development of NATO.

(c) Was fear of communism the most important factor in explaining Britain's foreign policy between 1945 and 1953? Explain your answer.

(15 marks)

How to answer this question

The best answers will be those that examine a range of relevant issues. Such answers need to show an understanding of the analytical demands of the question and, through a balanced explanation, arrive at a judgement. The key words in the question are 'most important'. The route to the answer is to examine Britain's fear of communism, particularly in Europe. You also need to consider the British objective of remaining an influential power in global politics and what strategies Britain adopted to achieve this. The answer should cover the whole period up to and including Britain's involvement in the Korean War. You also may conclude that fear of communism was a central issue in Britain's foreign policy thinking but less significant than Britain's wider global interests in a Cold War nuclear age.

ESSAY QUESTIONS IN THE STYLE OF OCR

Questions

Questions **a** and **b** below relate to British foreign and imperial policies, 1846–1902.

Before you answer question **a**, read Chapters 1–3 in this book.

This question carries 30 marks from a total of 90. The question paper is 60 minutes in duration so you should spend about twenty minutes answering it.

The key requirement in attaining a high mark in this type of question is that you **explain rather than describe** the **two** reasons you select for your answer. Include range and depth in your explanations and select relevant factual detail that supports your explanation. Do not simply include detail because you know it!

> (a) Explain **two** reasons to account for Britain's relations with Russia between 1846 and 1878. (30 marks)

How to answer this question

At the **planning stage**, you need to decide **what** the nature of Britain's relationship with Russia was during this period. This could include:

- Britain feared that Russia was expansionist. Britain feared that Russia wanted to expand westwards into Europe and also control the Mediterranean Sea
- Britain feared that Russia was willing to act aggressively and use any diplomatic and military means to achieve its expansionist objectives.

You also need to decide **why** Britain feared Russia. This could include:

- the threat Russia posed to the European balance of power
- the threat posed to British trade and links to the empire
- the economic consequences for Britain in addition to the threat to trade.

You also need to consider **how** Britain's relations with Russia were expressed during this period. This would include:

- the Crimean War: causes and events
- the Eastern Question, 1875–8.

Structure your answer so that **the arguments** are clear and the **supporting evidence** is focused and sufficient to back what you are saying. For example, having established that Britain feared Russian expansionism, you then need to illustrate Russian expansionism through the Crimean War, discuss how that could have threatened the balance of power and explain why the balance of power was so important to British interests. You need to develop the last part most fully. The balance of power meant stability and that meant peace; not expensive European wars. It guaranteed the security of Britain's status as a great power. Fear of expansionism also meant a fear of the threat to British trade and the security of the empire, particularly if Russia increased its influence in the Mediterranean. Reference could be made to Russia's expansionism into the Turkish Empire and Eastern Europe and how this could lead to greater influence in the Mediterranean. You need to explain why Russian influence in the region would damage British trade. The Eastern Mediterranean and the route to India are factors that are particularly worth developing here.

Before you answer question **b**, read Chapters 4 and 5.

As this question carries 60 marks from a total of 90, you should spend the remaining 40 minutes answering it. This suggests a more detailed and developed answer than for question **a**. The best answers will **evaluate** the key issues. This involves producing a critical analysis of the factors and making a comparative assessment of their relative importance. You need to establish whether **each individual reason** is a strong reason or not and **why**.

> (b) Why did the British people support the extension of the empire so enthusiastically during the period c.1880–1902? (60 marks)

How to answer this question
At the **planning stage**, the first task is to establish the range of factors. These could include:

- the impact of pro-imperialist propaganda through newspapers and other popular literature
- the role of popular entertainment
- the economic opportunities, business and employment
- popular patriotism and the support for Britain's role against its international rivals
- support for the missionary and 'civilising' roles of imperialism
- the role and influence of individuals, such as Joseph Chamberlain and Cecil Rhodes.

The **introductory paragraph** should outline what you intend to prove. It should not consist of generalised background detail. Focus on the question immediately and tell the reader what you intend to argue and briefly how you intend to do it. Avoid phrases such as 'In this essay, I intend to write about...' since this adds nothing to the answer and takes up time and space. Make every sentence add something to your argument. Avoid the mistake of 'bolting on' comments at the end of a paragraph of factual detail. Comments such as 'From this it can be seen that...' lack focus and analytical depth. The answer should be structured so that supporting evidence is used to reinforce the argument. An evaluation of the factors should lead to an assessment of their relative importance. Consider, for example, how the propaganda was delivered. Was it a calculated act of persuasion? What evidence of its effectiveness or ineffectiveness is there? Why did some groups oppose imperialism? Was imperialism economically beneficial to everyone? If not, why not, and what effect did this have on the notion of 'popular imperialism'?

You need to construct a clear **judgement** in the **concluding paragraph**. This should summarise the main arguments that you have established in the body of the answer. It should offer a balanced assessment of the relative importance of the range of factors you have used. Essentially, the conclusion should remind the reader that you have now proved what you stated as your intention in the introduction.

More questions

Questions **a** and **b** relate to British foreign and imperial policy between 1939 and 1963.

Before you answer question **a**, read Chapters 7, 8 and 10 in this book. It would also be useful to read the general comments concerning question **a** type questions outlined in the previous section.

> **(a)** Explain **two** reasons why Britain decolonised between 1945 and 1960.   (30 marks)

How to answer this question

There is no specific way to respond to this question, but there are a number of equally good routes to take. At the **planning stage**, you need to decide what approach you intend to take to this type of broad question. One route is to consider at least two colonies and examine the nature of their decolonisation. You could take decolonisation in India and Malaya, for example. Another route is to identify two significant contributors to decolonisation. These could include Macmillan and the 'wind of change' speech in 1960, the economic relationship Britain developed with the empire after 1945, or the economic relationship Britain developed with Europe. A further route is to consider a thematic approach. You could take the themes of nationalism and its impact on British policy, the theme of Britain's economic priorities after 1945, or the theme of Britain's strategic interests and the increasing irrelevancy of the empire in the post-war Cold War world.

Having established the basic route, it is then necessary to develop the relevant detail and **explain** how each factor contributed to decolonisation. Having considered the factors that contributed to Indian independence, you need to illustrate which was the **most significant**. Was it Indian nationalism, Britain's changed strategic priorities, economic factors, or some other factor? A detailed explanation of Macmillan's 'wind of change' might suggest that Britain was reacting to pan-African nationalism, or that it was a response to Britain's changed economic priorities, or the first open admission of the new realities for Britain in a post-Suez world. As stated at the start of this section, there are a wide variety of options and it is perfectly acceptable for you to 'mix and match' your approach. The key things are that your answer has a coherent structure, there is range and depth of relevant detail, there is a clear explanation of how and why the factors contributed to decolonisation, and you arrive at a conclusion that summarises the explanations.

Before answering question **b**, read Chapters 7, 9 and 10 of this book. It would also be useful to read the general comments relating to question **b** type questions outlined in the previous section.

> (b) 'It was for purely economic reasons that Britain refused to join the EEC in 1957 but had changed its mind by 1963.' How far do you agree with this view?   (60 marks)

How to answer this question

The first stage in the **planning** process is to establish what the range of factors are that motivated Britain's policies in 1957 and 1963. These could include:

- a long-standing reluctance to become part of an integrated Europe. This goes back to immediately after the Second World War
- reference could be made to the pre-1957 moves for greater economic cooperation through the ECSC. This could illustrate a degree of consistency in British policy, which led to the 1957 decision. Reference could be made to the issue of national sovereignty as a purely non-economic factor
- another important non-economic issue is the post-war strategic policy that Britain had developed. This was focused on a close strategic relationship with the USA rather than a purely regional European relationship
- emphasis could be placed on the relationship that Britain wanted with the Commonwealth. This went beyond simply an economic relationship as it encompassed strategic issues in terms of Britain's role as a post-war global power
- in 1957, Britain's thinking was to develop an alternative economic union that did not have wider implications for future political integration. Reference could be made to the EFTA here
- at this point, you need to consider what had changed by 1963 and why. You should look for evidence of both economic and non-economic factors. Macmillan's new thinking on Britain's relationship with the Commonwealth could be explored from an economic perspective. Strategic and political issues, such as the prospect of a Europe dominated by French influence and the pressure that Britain was under from the USA, are also directly relevant here. The USA's wider strategic, political and military interests in Europe form an important part of Britain's new thinking on Europe.

Having gathered the relevant information, the next task is to **structure** this into a **coherent** and **balanced analysis** that leads to a clearly defined **judgement**. A useful approach to self-criticism in essay writing is to have someone read your answer without knowing what the question was. A good essay that addresses the question directly should enable the reader to work out what the question was. If you cannot do this, then the answer either contains too much narrative, is too generalised, or includes too much irrelevant detail.

In this question, you should establish balance by examining the non-economic factors as well as the economic ones. You should also establish a clear judgement by showing whether economic issues were the most significant in both 1957 and 1963.

A2 SECTION: INTRODUCTION

Aspects of foreign policy and the rise and fall of the empire

The nineteenth century witnessed the rise of the British Empire and the twentieth century witnessed its fall. This section considers a policy direction that led to war in 1939 and, ultimately, to the decline of empire. The policy was appeasement. The Second World War contributed to the economic and strategic factors that shifted Britain's position and enabled colonial nationalism to become so effective in influencing Britain's policies.

SECTION 1

To what extent did public opinion force the British Government to follow a policy of appeasement in the 1930s? The key issue here is whether the government responded to public opinion or whether it manipulated it for political gain. To a large extent both processes were at work throughout the 1930s.

SECTION 2

How far do economic factors explain the acquisition, expansion and dismantling of Britain's empire? Economic factors were central to the development of Britain's empire. An analysis of this apparently obvious conclusion is undertaken in this section. Significantly, economic factors played a pivotal role in the dismantling of the empire.

SECTION 3

How significant were international relations in the rise and fall of Britain's empire? Strategic factors were always important determinants in Britain's policy decisions regarding its empire and the role the empire was to have in contributing to Britain's international status. This section examines the changes in those policies and analyses the reasons for the changes.

SECTION 4

To what extent did Britain's perception of its empire change over time? It is significant that, despite the popular image of the empire as a reflection of Britain's greatness, the empire was almost always treated in a purely pragmatic manner by successive British governments. When the empire ceased to offer any direct benefit to Britain it was simply expendable as it was no longer an asset.

SECTION 5

How valid is the view that colonial nationalism was the key to decolonisation? Nationalism took various forms and was a twentieth century phenomenon. It undoubtedly did influence British policy, but it was by no means as effective as it appeared to be. Its contribution was variable, and at times almost irrelevant to the British decolonisation policy.

SECTION 1

To what extent did public opinion force the British government to follow a policy of appeasement in the 1930s?

KEY PERSON

Neville Chamberlain (1869–1940) Chamberlain entered national politics as a Conservative Party MP in 1918. In the years 1924–9, he was Minister of Health in the Baldwin administration. His political reputation grew and he became Chancellor of the Exchequer in 1931 until he succeeded Baldwin as leader of the Conservative Party and became Prime Minister in 1937. He held the Premiership until 1940 when he resigned after the defeat of British forces in Norway. The high point of his policy of appeasement was reached in the Munich Agreement in 1938.

Appeasement was not the outcome of any one single factor. It was a policy that had begun in the 1920s, and it was driven by a belief in the ability of the victorious powers to cooperate successfully with Germany and to restore Germany into the family of European and world powers. There was an overwhelming commitment to avoiding another catastrophe like the Great War. Britain's economic condition and the need to protect the empire also figured largely in an apparent reluctance to strengthen Britain's defence systems and armed forces unnecessarily. Public opinion undoubtedly did play a significant role in policy formulation, at least until the mid-1930s. **Neville Chamberlain's** role was central to the whole process. He was a committed appeaser and understood the importance of not only reacting to public opinion but also shaping it for his own ends. Chamberlain's commitment to appeasement was pragmatic. He had little alternative but to follow appeasement since the only alternative was war and Britain was in no position to contemplate that in 1937.

HISTORICAL INTERPRETATION

In order to assess the extent to which public opinion influenced the government to follow a policy of appeasement, it is also necessary to consider the other factors that contributed to that policy. Appeasement has been at the centre of a controversial historical debate since the outbreak of the Second World War.

The first phase of historical research emerged almost immediately after the outbreak of war. It suggested that Britain was still a great power and had the resources to challenge Germany's aggression in Europe. Therefore to chose appeasement rather than resistance was to submit weakly to German aggression. A group of left-wing writers were amongst this first phase and included Michael Foot and Franck Owen. They used the collective pseudonym Cato to publish *Guilty Men* in 1940. This accused Chamberlain of deliberately manipulating public opinion by raising unrealistic hopes of peace with Germany. Chamberlain underestimated Britain's capacity to fight and overestimated Germany's. Essentially, Chamberlain is presented as the great deceiver. In 1948, Winston Churchill published *The Gathering Storm*. In this he reinforced the anti-appeasement judgements in *Guilty Men* and condemned Baldwin's failure to rearm as being motivated by political survival. Baldwin was accused of pandering to the public fear of war and allowing this to slow Britain's rearmament programme during the 1930s.

In 1961, A.J.P. Taylor, in *The Origins of the Second World War*, emphasised the pivotal role appeasement had taken in the outbreak of the Second World War: 'The cause of war was therefore as much the blunders of others as the wickedness of the dictators themselves.' Even in 1963, Martin Gilbert and Richard Gott, in *The Appeasers*, still argued that Chamberlain deceived the British public into accepting appeasement.

From the late 1960s, a new revisionist interpretation began to emerge. Revisionist historians emphasised the constraints that made appeasement the only viable policy for Britain to follow in the 1930s. Britain's defence capabilities were weak because its economy was weak and its imperial defence needs drained resources. Some historians, such as Patrick Finney, see appeasement as an almost inevitable consequence of Britain's decline. Revisionists also emphasise the influential role of public opinion before 1937. Maurice Cowling, in *The Impact of Hitler: British Politics and British Policy, 1933–40* (1975), argues that appeasement was driven primarily by domestic considerations. The economy, the empire and the political control of the Conservative Party motivated Chamberlain to pursue a policy that would be popular with the British public. This interpretation of motives seems to make public opinion crucial in influencing Chamberlain. Public opinion was monitored through a limited number of opinion polls, particularly in the months following the Munich Agreement. Chamberlain even shifted away from his established position in March 1939 in response to public opinion pressure after the German occupation of Prague. Chamberlain is presented as a responsible leader sensitive to the opinions of the British people.

In 1981, Paul Kennedy summarised research on the domestic influences that contributed to the shaping of appeasement policy in his work *The Realities Behind Diplomacy*. In this, for example, Kennedy argues that Chamberlain responded very positively to the public criticism of Germany after the Prague coup in March 1939. Public opinion had a direct influence on government thinking. The 1980s saw yet another interpretive focus. R.A.C. Parker, in *Chamberlain and Appeasement* (1993), presents Chamberlain as a dominant and ruthless political influence but suggests it was not Britain's economic and military weaknesses that motivated his actions. Parker argues that Chamberlain was profoundly committed to appeasement and was willing to use whatever means were necessary to create a supportive general public. Positive public support was an essential pre-requisite for appeasement to exist but public support was not an end in itself. Public support did not initiate and prolong appeasement; it was appeasement and the great appeaser, Chamberlain, which created the support. There is some consensus between revisionists and so-called counter revisionists in that they seem to agree that Chamberlain both responded to and manipulated public opinion.

HOW DOES PUBLIC OPINION WORK IN A DEMOCRACY?

The idea that the government's foreign goals and diplomatic actions are primarily a response to public opinion, or that public opinion is virtually ignored by governments when they determine such goals and actions, are equally misleading. Another issue is the extent to which governments deliberately manipulate public opinion in order to ensure that the opinion is supportive of already determined government policy decisions. The levels of knowledge and interest that different groups within the general public hold varies considerably, but studies have shown that the great majority of people hold some view about foreign policy goals.

Gabriel Almond, in his work *The American People and Foreign Policy* (1977), produced findings that are valid in any modern and developed democracy. Almond suggested that there was a 'foreign policy mood' amongst the general public. In Britain, in the 1930s, the mood was one of war weariness. The mood did not translate into actual foreign policy objectives but it did set limits that policy-makers had to take note of. In Almond's argument, it would have been impossible for Neville Chamberlain to pursue an aggressive and warlike policy because that would have ignored the public mood of pacifism. There were numerous demonstrations from the mid-1930s demanding the formulation of government policy that would lead to the preservation of peace. Pacifistic undergraduate demonstrations were relatively common. The government's task was to develop policies and actions that the British public could make sense of and support. In 1938, Chamberlain was the most popular Prime Minister of modern times because he did exactly that at the Munich Conference. The mood of the British public had a constraining effect on policy alternatives but had only a limited effect on specific policy decisions. Almond's argument is that the Chamberlain government understood the mood of the people, but while that mood had an insignificant impact on actual decisions, it did set some parameters within which those decisions were made. War had to be avoided, if it was possible, and the policy had to reflect that mood.

In his work *International Politics: A Framework for Analysis,* 7th Edn. (1994), K.J. Holsti argues that governments do not simply respond to public pressure, they often actually create it.

Because of superior knowledge and access to information, governments occupy a position from which they can interpret reality to the population and actually create attitudes, opinions, and images where none existed before...Thus, what many people know of, or feel about, a critical situation abroad and their own government's actions and responses may originate from the government itself.

Press conferences, political speeches and parliamentary debates all act as vehicles to enable government to influence public opinion rather than merely react to it. Public opinion is not shaped solely through government tactics; it is also influenced by the media, which in turn may be directly or indirectly influenced by the government.

THE MASS MEDIA: MANIPULATOR OF OPINION OR MERELY ITS REFLECTOR?

Britain's mass media in the 1930s may be regarded as the press, the radio and the cinema industry. Although the media may reflect public opinion, it may also become a vital tool in the hands of a government that wishes to manipulate public opinion. The media was essentially a tool in the hands of the government. Its role was not merely to manipulate opinion in Britain, but also to promote government policy. The media was a vehicle which the government could exploit in order to give the impression that the majority of the British people supported its policies towards Germany. The media in general had more to gain from supporting the government than by opposing it. There were clear examples of newspapers that did not back Chamberlain's government and Low's anti-appeasement cartoons in the *Evening Standard* bear clear testimony to that. A popular government policy reported and backed by a newspaper made that publication popular with the general public. The mood of the public was undoubtedly in favour of peace, and appeasement appeared to offer that. Therefore, if the media, particularly the press, wanted to court the support of the British people, it had to back appeasement, and that meant forming an alliance with the government. Equally, the government was determined to use all its power to ensure that the media acted as a voice that justified government policies. Commercially, the media was in no position to challenge the mood of the people by damning appeasement.

The government held variable levels of control over the different elements of the media, particularly the press. Within the media there was a range of political opinion. Some elements were dominated by the left, while others were the natural followers of Chamberlain and Conservatism. The media as a whole had no coordinated or concerted agenda that it was determined to fulfil. These divisions served to strengthen the government's ability to exploit the media for its own purposes.

The press

Both national and regional newspapers generally supported appeasement. *The Times* was one of the best-selling national newspapers of the 1930s and it was committed to appeasement. Geoffrey Dawson, the editor of *The Times*, expressed the line his paper took on appeasement when he wrote:

> *Personally I am, and always have been, anxious that we should explore every avenue in search of a reasonable understanding with Germany…I do my utmost night and day to keep out of the paper anything that might hurt their [Germany's] susceptibilities…I have always been convinced that the peace of the world depends more than anything on our getting on better relations with Germany.*

A cartoon entitled 'Still Hope' published in 1938 in the magazine Punch

In his work *The Times and the Appeasement of Hitler* (1974), Colin Seymour-Ure concludes that 'Dawson's connections…were so interwoven with the politics of the day that it would be impossible to estimate who influenced whom'. In *Rearmament and the British Public: Policy and Propaganda* (1987), N. Pronay emphasises the attitudes held by major national newspapers during the 1930s when he notes that they saw themselves as 'the makers and arbiters of both party and government'. For Pronay, the press was pivotal in promoting government policy but also in contributing to its development. The press conducted a service for the government in that it used its position to advertise and legitimise government policy, but it also had the opportunity to shape that policy in return for the service it offered government. The press reinforced the government's justification for appeasement by emphasising the moral right of Germany to recover its lost territories and reunite its people. It also emphasised the danger from air attack and the limitations of Britain's ability to defend itself against a vengeful Germany. There was almost a symbiotic relationship between press and government in the 1930s.

Although this symbiosis existed, it was not absolute. In 1938, Sir Joseph Ball sent a secret memorandum to Chamberlain, which illustrated the somewhat tenuous support that the press gave and the limitations of government influence over the press. The memo noted:

> *Although a number of national dailies are nominally supporters of the government, none of them can be relied upon for full, continuous and deliberately planned support…Indeed, some of them deliberately adopt, from time to time, the role of 'candid' friend.*

During the Munich crisis, the *Daily Herald*, the *Daily Telegraph* and the *News Chronicle* all demanded firmer action against Germany and its allies. After the German occupation of Prague in March 1939, there was a wave of popular discontent and this was mirrored in traditional pro-Conservative newspapers, such as *The Observer*.

Radio

In 1927, the BBC became a corporation and it was led by the Director General, John Reith. Its authority was granted through a Royal Charter. The so-called 'Reithian Trinity' was the foundation for a public service based on information, education and entertainment. This apparent openness and objectivity was dangerous to the government. The BBC could not be depended upon to act as a mouthpiece for government policy. As many people listened to the radio as read newspapers and, in many ways, the radio was a more 'user friendly' medium for ordinary people. Essentially, the Royal Charter gave the BBC a massive degree of independence from government influence. The BBC had no vested interest that it needed to protect by cooperating with the government.

In 1937, the government tried to persuade Reith to bring in more right-wing staff because, as a civil servant noted, 'nearly nine out of every ten in the BBC are left'. The government's actions in 1938 clearly illustrate the importance it placed on radio and its determination to enhance its influence over this vital medium. Since Reith was the basis of the problem, Chamberlain simply removed him from the BBC. The charter guaranteed the BBC's authority but it did not guarantee the Director General's security of tenure. Reith's successor was the pro-government appointee, Sir Richard Maconachie. Despite these changes, the BBC retained some of its independence and Reith's all-pervasive influence remained intact to some extent.

Cinema

Most people went to the cinema at least twice a week. It was a popular national pastime in an age before the mass ownership of televisions. Thus, the cinema was a potent form of information and attitude formation and it had the power to shape opinions. No lesser person than Joseph Goebbels, the Nazi Minister of Popular Enlightenment and Propaganda, had already realised this in Germany. This reality was not lost on the government's thinking. The government did have the means to control what the general public saw in cinemas. In the late 1920s, the British Board of Film Censors (BBFC) was created by the government. By 1934, the BBFC had total control over what would be contained in a film, even if a film would be released for general viewing.

There was an obsessive fear of aerial bombing. The general public was convinced that this would be a key feature of any new war and therefore something had to be done to prevent this. Alexander Korda's production of H.G. Wells' *Things to Come*, in 1936, heightened these fears. Such films were the product of an astute film industry exploiting public anxiety in order to heighten viewing figures and profits. There is little evidence of any attempt to shape opinion on the part of the industry at this level. The government backed the BBFC in its promotion of such films in order to create a public mood that would reinforce any anti-war policy.

Another form of the genre was the documentary film. A leading figure in this genre was John Grierson. He condemned feature filmmakers for making 'war more exciting than peace'. Grierson was, according to Pronay, of 'a soft-left and anti-war disposition'. In *Documentary and Educational Films of the 1930s* (1979), Rachel Low argues that Grierson 'theorised about the need for an education for democracy'. Clearly the documentary filmmakers wanted to stimulate thought about government policy and the international situation. Documentary filmmakers like Grierson supported appeasement, but their primary motive was pacifism rather than buying time for rearmament. The films continued to promote the objectives of the government in terms of manipulating and formulating public opinion. In 1936, Paul Rotha, a close friend of Grierson, made a short film designed to stimulate opposition to the government's rearmament plans. The primary aim of the documentary filmmakers was to educate the public about the horror of war and to reinforce the quest for disarmament and a commitment to collective security. The motives that drove the documentary filmmakers were very different from those of the press barons, but they performed an equally important role in shaping public opinion.

Documentary filmmakers saw film as a form of education and the means by which the public could be informed of the horrors of bombing, for example, in a factual way. The press was geared more to political alignments, either for or against government policy. Certainly, before rearmament began to gather pace, the documentary filmmakers were staunch, albeit unintentional, allies of the government.

A third form of film also existed: this was the newsreel. These provided news and current affair summaries shown in cinemas. The owners of the newsreel companies were similar in their attitudes to those of the press barons. These owners and the politicians had much in common and exploited this mutually beneficial relationship. The government could restrict access to state occasions so the newsreels cooperated in reinforcing government objectives. There are numerous examples of newsreel footage presenting Chamberlain as a man of peace and the only man who could save the country from war. The bombing of Guernica and Barcelona during the Spanish Civil War offered significant opportunities for the government to exploit the public fear of aerial bombing. A classic example of the newsreel being used as a vehicle for government propaganda came when Chamberlain was returning from the Munich Conference by air. Chamberlain's voice was superimposed over a view of London below. He expressed his firm belief that Britain was vulnerable from the air and that the defence of Czechoslovakia was secondary to the broader interests of international peace and thus continued to reinforce the justification for government policies. The development of **air defences** and the expansion of the Royal Air Force were underway, but at a relatively slow pace. The expansion came when there was a growing perception that war was a real possibility.

PUBLIC OPINION POLLS

Professionally structured public opinion polls were first used in Britain in 1937, although polls had been carried out before this. During the 1930s, appeasement developed, particularly from 1937, when Chamberlain became Prime Minister. The polls are good indicators of opinion and they are useful when determining how closely synchronised the development of public opinion was with the development of government policy.

In July 1935, the League of Nations Union, a group committed to disarmament and collective security through international cooperation, held the 'Peace Ballot'. 11 million people participated in the ballot. The results illustrate some significant indicators of public opinion in 1935.

Question: Should Britain remain a member of the League of Nations?
Yes: 10,642,560 (97%) No: 337,000 (3%)

Question: Are you in favour of an all-round reduction in armaments by international agreement?
Yes: 10,058,000 (92.5%) No: 815,365 (7.5%)

Question: Do you consider that if a nation insists on attacking another, the other nations should combine to compel it to stop by economic and non-military measures?
Yes: 9,627,606 (94.1%) No: 607,165 (5.9%)

Question: Do you consider that if a nation insists on attacking another, the other nations should combine to stop it by, if necessary, military measures?
Yes: 6,506,777 (74.2%) No: 2,262,261 (25.8%)

Air defences
During the 1930s the emphasis was on bomber development, but there were also improvements in fighter defences with the development of the Spitfire. Ground defences were also improved through the work done on radars as an early warning system. Barrage balloons were recycled from the First World War and designed to keep bombers high and therefore less accurate. Anti-aircraft artillery was also developed, although it was more effective as a deterrent than as a way of accurately targeting enemy aircraft.

The data clearly suggests that there was an overwhelming commitment to multilateral disarmament and collective security as the basis for international relations. The respondents backed a non-military form of collective security, but the greater majority were willing to accept a military solution if all else failed. Thus peace, disarmament and collective security appeared to permeate the national mentality in 1935. Ironically, as the response to the final question illustrates, how could Britain contribute to a form of military collective security and at the same time disarm? Did government policy up to 1935 reflect this mood and if so, was this the result of mass public opinion successfully moulding policy or would the government have taken the course it did anyway? The evidence would suggest that Britain's policy, before the emergence of Chamberlain as Prime Minister, appeared to be consistent with the mood of popular opinion, but this was more apparent than real.

DEFENCE

An analysis of government policies in the 1920s and into the 1930s reveals quite clearly that the government was not reacting to public pressure and the public mood but to very specific factors that made policy outcomes very focused, but focused in such a manner that they appeared to share the emotive response of the public towards some form of controlled pacifism and disarmament.

The First World War had brought an eleven-fold increase in the National Debt by 1918. Annual interest payments amounted to almost 40 per cent of government spending in 1920. In this situation, defence spending cuts were almost inevitable and this approach continued into the 1930s. In 1919, the armed services were instructed to assume 'that the British Empire will not be engaged in any great war during the next ten years, and that no expeditionary force is required for that purpose'. This was the basis of the 'Ten Year Rule'. In effect, the reasoning was that if no war threatened Britain, then there was no need to expand the armed forces and Britain's defence capacity. The Ten Year Rule remained in place until March 1932 after Japan attacked Manchuria. When Germany left the Geneva Disarmament Conference and the League of Nations in October 1933, Britain began to assess its defence requirements. It was at this point that government policy appeared to deviate from popular opinion.

Even though public opinion supported disarmament, a rearmament programme was begun from mid-1934. Public opinion was not directing government policy. The Defence Requirements Committee (DRC) identified Germany as 'the ultimate potential enemy' and recommended a balanced rearmament programme. It was at this point that public attitudes did appear to shape significantly the nature of rearmament. The focus of rearmament was to be the development of a bomber force at the expense of the development of the other services. Bombers were seen as the most cost-effective option at the time. The government adopted an air programme well in excess of Air Ministry requests.

It must be emphasised that a major constraint on the development of the other services alongside the air force was fiscal restraint. There were simply not the economic resources to rearm as the government wished and in line with the DRC recommendations. In 1931, there was a deficit of £104 million. Exports and invisible earnings declined as the world economic depression hit Britain. Hence, the government did respond in a controlled way to public opinion because it could not deliver the scale of rearmament that was needed.

APPEASEMENT UNDER CHAMBERLAIN

Public opinion poll data offers an interesting insight into the mood of the British people during the critical period of March 1938 to April 1939. The period marks the demise of appeasement as the cornerstone of British foreign policy.

> **Question:** Should Britain promise assistance to Czechoslovakia if Germany acts as it did towards Austria? (Asked March 1938)
> Yes: 33% No: 43% No opinion: 24%
>
> **Question:** Hitler says he has no more territorial ambitions in Europe. Do you believe him? (Asked October 1938)
> Yes: 7% No: 93%
>
> **Question:** Which of these views comes closest to your views of Chamberlain's policy of appeasement? (Asked February 1939)
> 1. It is a policy that will ultimately lead to a lasting peace in Europe: 28%
> 2. It will keep us out of war until we have time to rearm: 46%
> 3. It is bringing war nearer by whetting the appetite of the dictators: 24%
> 4. No opinion: 2%
>
> **Question:** Is the British government right in following a policy giving guarantees to preserve the independence of small European states? (Asked April 1939)
> Yes: 83% No: 17%

Chamberlain came into office as Prime Minister in May 1937. In March 1938, Germany annexed Austria. The first real crisis Chamberlain faced after this was over the fate of Czechoslovakia.

MUNICH, 1938

In December 1937, Sir Thomas Inskip presented a major review of defence policy. This prioritised Britain's defence needs and placed the defence of Britain from air attacks as a top priority, followed by the protection of Britain's colonies and trade. Any form of European involvement was the lowest priority. This report was put to the test in September 1938 when Germany demanded the Sudetenland from Czechoslovakia. Chamberlain had already decided, in March 1938, that Britain would offer no help to the Czechs. Clearly there was a consistency between public opinion and government policy. The great majority appeared to support Chamberlain's policy. Chamberlain's radio broadcast on the evening of 27 September 1938, when the Czech crisis was at its height, clearly illustrates Chamberlain's skill in manipulating public opinion in his favour. He cleverly appealed to popular fears that he knew existed amongst the British public when he said:

> *How horrible, fantastic, incredible it is that we should be digging trenches and trying on gas masks here because of a quarrel in a far-away country between people of whom we know nothing...War is a fearful thing, and we must be very clear, before we embark on it, that it is really the great issues that are at stake.*

Chamberlain reinforced this popular support by declaring that he had secured 'peace in our time'. However, the mood of public euphoria began to change fairly rapidly and with it government policy.

The most fundamental shift in British policy came not immediately after Munich but between January and April 1939. The public also reflected the view that Hitler's expansionist ambitions had not been satisfied at Munich. The final turning point came on 15 March 1939 when Hitler seized the rest of the Czech lands. In his book *The Realities Behind Diplomacy* (1981), Paul Kennedy notes:

> *The explosion of discontent which followed, in the Conservative Party and in the traditional pro-government papers like* The Observer, *forced a sudden change of tone; by 17 March, Chamberlain was publicly warning that 'any attempt to dominate the world by force was one which the democracies must resist'.*

The public was no longer prepared to accept Hitler as a man to be trusted. Prague unearthed a national sense of humiliation and anger. The Conservative Party was also demanding a change of policy. Lord Halifax, the Foreign Secretary, was a prime mover in this process. Chamberlain knew that 1940 was to be an election year. Despite this, the significance of domestic politics should not be exaggerated.

The government orchestrated a major shift in policy. On 29 March, it announced that the Territorial Army was to be doubled in size and a month later a conscription bill was introduced into Parliament. By April, Britain had committed itself to guaranteeing the security of Eastern Europe, through Poland, Greece and Romania. The question is, were these changes a direct response to public opinion and the attitudes within the Conservative Party? The measures may be regarded as political manoeuvres to placate the French. As Sir John Simon, the Chancellor of the Exchequer, observed, 'We are not preparing for war, we are constructing a peace front'. The government still believed that it could avoid war. No clear military planning had gone into either of the decisions referred to above. Clearly there were a number of motivational factors underlying these decisions. They were designed to reinforce the French, deter Hitler, and respond positively to public opinion in Britain.

CONCLUSIONS

Establishing the extent to which public policy is directly or indirectly influenced by public opinion is always a difficult process. In terms of the 1930s, it was made even more difficult through the relative lack of substantive data. Opinion polls were not held with any regularity, certainly not until towards the end of the decade. Thus the evidence base is limited. Governments had to respond to public opinion, particularly when that opinion was so firmly fixed against another war as a result of the experience of the carnage in the First World War. The policy of appeasement was certainly one that the government could confidently deliver knowing that it would have widespread popular support. However, it would be wrong to conclude that the government had unconditional backing from the public. Governments were compelled to manipulate the support, particularly when it became obvious that some degree of rearmament was inevitable. This process of manipulation can be traced through the relationship governments had with much of the press and certainly through the powerful visual imagery of the film newsreel.

SECTION 2

How far do economic factors explain the acquisition, expansion and dismantling of Britain's empire?

Economic imperialism is an idea that has interested historians since the beginning of the twentieth century. It is an appealing argument to suggest that the British Empire developed in order that it might act as a convenient source of raw materials for British industry and markets for British manufactured goods. It is equally appealing to argue that the empire declined when it became an economic burden rather than an economic asset to Britain.

In some parts of the empire, economic factors undoubtedly played a crucial role in imperial control. In many parts of the empire, economic factors played only a secondary role. The economic advantages of empire have been grossly overestimated. The reality was that, often, imperial possessions were costing more to maintain than the income and economic opportunities they generated for Britain and imperial investors.

The process of decolonisation, although founded partly on an economic rationale, was as much the product of nationalism and changed strategic priorities as economic necessity. To suggest that the empire was simply too costly to maintain and therefore must be dismantled misses the broader context in which political decisions were taken. It also misrepresents the political and economic objectives begun under Macmillan and continued into the 1970s. Despite this, economic pragmatism did contribute significantly to decolonisation after 1945.

HISTORICAL INTERPRETATION: ACQUISITION AND EXPANSION

Economic issues have, for the last twenty years, been the focal point of historical debate on British imperialism. The period between 1870 and 1914 has often been referred to as an age of 'New Imperialism'. It was during this period that the empire expanded most rapidly, particularly in Africa and Asia. Historians have devoted considerable attention to the economic motives underlying British imperialism in this early period. One of the earliest interpretations came from J.A. Hobson in his work *Imperialism: A Study* (1902). Hobson's explanation rests on the surplus capital theory. The gap between rich and poor in Britain led to domestic under-consumption that prompted investors to put their surplus capital abroad. Imperial expansion occurred because the investors demanded that government protect their investments. As Hobson commented, 'finance is...the governor of the imperial engine, directing the energy and determining the work.' Lenin took the view a stage further and argued in *Imperialism: The Highest Stage of Capitalism* (1916) that the capitalist economies must inevitably turn to imperialism in order to guarantee markets and supplies of raw materials. Capital had to go abroad or capitalism itself would stagnate.

By the 1950s, revisionist historians began to challenge the received understanding of the economic arguments for imperialism. In 1953, R. Robinson and J. Gallagher, in *The Imperialism of Free Trade*, argued that Britain developed an 'informal' empire through free trade agreements with weak states that did not actually become part of the 'formal' British Empire. This they referred to as the 'imperialism of free trade'. The same historians, in 1961, produced *Africa and the Victorians: The Official Mind of Imperialism*. In this they argued for India's centrality in British imperial thinking. Britain participated in the colonisation of Africa in order to protect trading interests with India. In this way, economic factors have a consequential rather than a direct causal role in imperial expansion.

By the 1980s, further developments had taken place in historical interpretation. Davis and Huttenback, in *Mammon and the Pursuit of Empire: The Political Economy of British Imperialism, 1860–1912* (1986), concluded that empire offered economic benefits for only a small elite. E. Hobsbawm added to the debate in 1994 with *The Age of Empire, 1875–1914*. He argued that up to 1914 imperial expansion was the result of the need for new markets and raw materials. In effect, it was the industrialists and the manufacturers who acted as the driving force in imperial development. P.J. Cain and A.G. Hopkins, in *British Imperialism: Innovation and Expansion, 1688–1914* (1993) and the 1998 work, *Gentlemanly Capitalism and British Imperialism: The New Debate on Empire*, challenged the economic interpretation that stressed the importance of manufacturing interests on imperial expansion. They argue that financial and service sectors, focused on Britain's financial centre, the City of London and the south east of England, exploited their links with political leaders at a time when finance and services were expanding. Here the economic argument is based on the centrality of the influence of the City.

ECONOMIC INFLUENCES UP TO 1914

The historiography suggests two basic economic forces that may have contributed significantly to the acquisition and expansion of the empire after 1870. The focus of this expansion was on the continent of Africa. The two arguments rest on the centrality of a specific economic factor. These are the centrality of the City and the centrality of trade and manufacturing. The question is, to what extent did one or both of these economic factors contribute to the acquisition and expansion of the empire between about 1870 and 1914?

The City

Essentially, the City was the financial heart of Britain. It consisted of the banks, investment houses, insurance companies and shipping firms. The principal objective of financial investment is to make a profit through offering financial aid to economic activities or by lending money to finance such activity. The notion that financial investment was a stimulus for imperial expansionism assumes that all parts of the empire that were acquired after 1870 were profitable investments that the investors strongly influenced government policy regarding imperial expansion and that there was a form of patriotism at work through the investments.

It is significant that between 1880 and 1914, the heyday of imperial expansionism, almost three quarters of British overseas investment was placed in the USA, Canada and Latin America, with only 25 per cent going to the empire. Patriotism was very much a secondary virtue compared to the profit motive. The aim of financiers was to achieve the best possible return on their investments and that was clearly to be achieved through non-imperial ventures. This distancing of the financial world from imperial activities suggests a limited commitment to the empire and therefore a limited influence over its expansion and development.

An analysis of the geographical distribution of investment also sheds light on the influence investors had in imperial expansion. Between 1887 and 1913, investment in Africa averaged about six per cent of the total overseas investment commitment. It averaged about ten per cent in India and about 22 per cent in the Dominions during the same period. The most recently expanded part of the empire received the smallest amount of investment. This hardly suggests that financial investment drove imperial expansion. Despite this, there were some parts of Africa that did attract considerable investment. The discovery of gold and diamonds in Cape Colony and the Boer Republics certainly generated investment in Southern Africa. Egypt was also an important area for financial investment. The Suez Canal attracted a large injection of British investment. Alexandria developed as a major port and a rail infrastructure was established. By 1879, Egypt had accrued debts of £100 million and entered into a debt crisis. Nationalist revolts in 1882 heightened the grave concerns of British investors to the point where the government was pressurised into establishing direct rule over Egypt. The City did put pressure on the government, but the decision to control Egypt was also driven by political and strategic factors. To a large extent, the interests of investors and the government were reciprocal and therefore the government was willing to act in the interests of finance. Strategic and political factors also determined government policy towards Egypt. Much of the rest of Africa attracted comparatively little investment as is illustrated from an article in *The Economist* from 1890:

> *The lands of tropical Africa are not suitable for a European population, and present inhabitants are races which it must take a far longer time to civilise than those who look for immediate big results appear to think of. We do not look for any rapid development of…financial success from these territories.*

The largest share of imperial investment went to the white settler Dominions. Although there were examples of high financial returns, many of the investments yielded lower profits than domestic ventures. Again, this reinforces the view that the influence of the City, in terms of its ability to promote imperial expansion, was limited. The City had a financial interest only in those areas of the empire that were potentially profitable, and this was very limited throughout much of Africa.

Trade and industry

Africa was undoubtedly an important source of raw materials for British industry. The Niger region of West Africa supplied palm oil, rubber and cocoa. These resources underpinned the soap, tinplate, tyre, electrical insulation and chocolate industries in Britain. It was trade in these commodities that had first linked Britain to West Africa. Government was able to appease the industrialists and avoid a direct imperial commitment by undertaking imperialism by proxy. The chartered trading companies committed themselves to maintain order, while the British government agreed to protect the trade from foreign aggression. The Royal Niger Company is a good example of this process at work. Government was cooperating with industry rather than being driven by its needs. The British government was reacting to the growing involvement in Africa from French and German trading interests and therefore its actions were reactive rather than proactive in West Africa.

From about 1870, Britain faced growing competition in world trade from Germany and the USA. Between 1870 and 1900, exports to those countries declined from 41 per cent to 30 per cent. Imperial trade did fill this gap to some extent. In 1875, 26 per cent of all Britain's exports went to the empire. By 1914, this had reached 35 per cent. However, Britain's share of the total trade with the empire actually declined during the same period. Clearly the empire was not a cushion to British trade and industry. What undermined this trade was Britain's commitment to a free trade policy. This, therefore, offers another explanation – that the influence of

British industry was limited. Indeed, there was no commitment on the part of industry to promote imperial protectionist policies of the sort later advocated by Joseph Chamberlain.

Joseph Chamberlain: the economic imperialist

As Colonial Secretary between 1895 and 1903, Chamberlain had an imperial vision that extended beyond a solely economic union within the empire to one where economic unity was at the heart of it. He was convinced that Britain and the empire would grow stronger by removing the free trade policies that currently existed and establishing intra-colonial preferential tariffs. He commented:

> If by adherence to economic pedantry…we are to lose opportunities of closer union which are offered by our colonies, if we put aside occasions now within our grasp, if we do not take every chance in our power to keep British trade in British hands, I am certain we shall deserve the disasters which will infallibly come upon us.

He saw the empire as a market for British goods that should not be readily shared with Britain's trading competitors. There was some support amongst the business community but it was insufficient to give Chamberlain the political strength he needed within the Unionist Party to push his plans through. Free trade was more important than imperial preference. Britain's world far outstripped its imperial trade and the economic arguments to abandon free trade simply weren't strong enough. Once again, economic issues were not driving imperial policy.

THE FIRST WORLD WAR: AN ECONOMIC TURNING POINT FOR THE EMPIRE?

The war had a profound economic impact on Britain. Profitable export markets were lost and Britain emerged from the war as a debtor nation, primarily to the USA. Trade with the empire had also declined because of the war. Economically, the First World War was a turning point because it marked a much closer economic relationship with the empire than had previously existed. The empire was perceived as an economic lifeline that Britain could call upon to cushion the economic impact of the war. During the war, the Dominions had been the most effective of Britain's colonial possessions in developing alternative trade links. For example, Canada had established important links with the USA through the export of agricultural products. This process continued to some extent after the war, but Britain made a concerted effort to restore the economic status quo. In the interwar years, Britain's imperial trade, particularly with the Dominions, increased significantly.

	Percentage of imperial imports into Britain	Percentage of exports from Britain into the empire
1910–14	25	36
1920–4	27	37
1925–9	28	42
1930–4	31	42
1935–9	39.5	49

Many Conservatives regarded imperial trade as a solution to Britain's post-war economic problems and many favoured the introduction of tariff controls to protect imperial trade from foreign competition. Only in 1932 did Britain finally abandon its free trade policy.

Although the war did reinforce the economic links between Britain and the empire, it was the Depression, which began in 1929, that really forced Britain to tighten its economic bond with its colonies. At the Imperial Economic Conference in Ottawa in 1932, agreements were set up for imperial preference. These agreements enabled preferential trade arrangements to be established between Britain and the Dominions and between the Dominions themselves. All such trade would be protected from foreign competition through the imposition of high tariffs. The policy helped the Dominions but actually worsened Britain's balance of payments position. After 1932, the percentage increase in imperial imports was greater than the increase in British exports to the empire. Despite this, these trade agreements did serve to reinforce imperial unity.

THE ECONOMICS OF DECOLONISATION AFTER 1945

Britain emerged from the Second World War with enormous debts, mostly incurred through borrowing money from the USA. In 1945 alone, Britain borrowed $3.75 billion from the USA. A condition of this loan was that sterling must become freely convertible with the dollar by 1947. In effect, this would have opened up imperial markets to the USA. To add to Britain's economic crisis, the rapidly developing Cold War demanded high levels of defence spending. Faced with these ever increasing economic constraints and the rise of nationalism throughout the empire, the logical option for Britain was to reduce costs through decolonisation. However, Britain did not experience a wave of decolonisation despite the crises in India and Palestine in 1947–8. Between 1948 and 1960, only three British colonies gained their independence. These were the Sudan (1956), the Gold Coast (1957) and Malaya (1957). Britain adopted a policy of colonial economic efficiency with a view to tightening its economic links with the empire.

Why colonial development and not mass decolonisation?

Central to Britain's economic priorities after 1945 was the sterling area. This was rigorously controlled after 1945 and developed very rapidly into a means of earning dollars for Britain. Some colonies, such as Malaya and the Gold Coast, had established very lucrative markets in the USA and had become important dollar earners. Britain bought the dollars and credited the colonies with sterling. In effect, the sterling area system protected the value of the pound and strengthened Britain's balance of payments position. Thus the colonies became an essential part of the sterling area. The possibility of Britain granting widespread independence to the non-dominion members of the sterling area was remote because they were too valuable economically. As Krozewski comments in *Sterling, The 'Minor' Territories and the End of Formal Empire, 1939–58* (1993), 'In the late 1940s and early 1950s, the empire was the backbone of the whole sterling area, largely because it was there that Britain could impose monetary and financial policies through political control'. The possibility of colonial nationalists taking control raised the spectre of sterling balances being drained. Such a course could have led to the British economy being destabilised and threatened with inflation. Britain's post-war dollar shortage was to be addressed by stimulating colonial exports to the USA and that meant colonial development. In a speech to the African Governors' Conference in November 1947, Sir Stafford Cripps, the Minister for Economic Affairs, reinforced this approach when he said:

> *It is the urgency of the present situation and the need for the Sterling Group and Western Europe both of them to maintain their economic independence that makes it so essential that we should increase out of all recognition the tempo of African development. We must be prepared to change our outlook and our habits of colonial development so that within the next two to five years we can get a really marked increase of production in coal, minerals, timber, raw materials of all kinds, and foodstuffs, and anything else that will save dollars or will sell in a dollar market.*

The Colonial Development Corporation (CDC)

In 1948, the CDC was formed with the aim, according to the Colonial Secretary, Arthur Creech Jones, of promoting 'in every possible way increased colonial production on an economic and self-supporting basis with an eye to the production of foodstuffs, raw materials and manufacturers whose supply to the UK or sales overseas will assist our balance of payments'. The scale of the government's commitment to colonial development may be seen through the 45 per cent increase in staffing levels in the Colonial Office between 1945 and 1948.

Thus Britain's immediate post-war colonial strategy was closely geared to economic factors that demanded the retention of colonial control rather than its relinquishment. The colonies were to provide cheap food and raw materials and absorb British manufactured goods. A classic example of this policy in action, and the policy failing, may be seen through the groundnut plan. A scheme was devised to mass produce groundnuts (peanuts) in Tanganika and 2.5 million acres of scrub was to be cleared. The plan later expanded into a more ambitious venture extending to Kenya and Rhodesia. Ultimately it was a disasterous failure and faced £49 million losses. The focal point of Britain's economic relationship with its colonies was the sterling area. All this necessitated tighter controls over the imperial economy than ever before. Economic exploitation rather than decolonisation was the primary agenda for Britain's relationship with the colonies in the decade following the Second World War. Nowhere more than Malaya illustrates the lengths to which Britain was prepared to go when the economic gains were worthwhile. In 1948, Malaya's net dollar earnings amounted to $170 million. Faced with communist terrorism in Malaya, Britain declared a state of emergency and spent the next five years destroying the terrorists. Increasingly, Britain's economic domination of its colonies was leading towards a critical state, as Fieldhouse notes in *The Labour Governments and the Empire–Commonwealth, 1945–51* (1984):

> *Between 1945 and 1951, Britain exploited those dependencies that were politically unable to defend their own interests in more ways and with more serious consequences than at any time since overseas colonies were established.*

Costs, benefits and economic change

By the late 1950s, the attempts to make the colonies an economic asset had failed. The failure simply added momentum to the demand for decolonisation that was coming from both the colonies and within Britain itself. The perceived economic benefits of decolonisation were becoming greater than the economic benefits of maintaining an empire. The key issues here are the extent to which the post-war strategy of colonial economic development accelerated decolonisation and the significance of economic factors in the decolonisation process.

By the mid-1950s, it had become increasingly clear that colonial economic potential was lacking. The economic gains simply did not warrant the investment. The policy of colonial economic development was largely an experiment that failed, but one that did not lead inevitably to a decolonisation alternative. The policy did heighten a sense of economic exploitation amongst nationalists, but it did not provoke a fundamental shift in British thinking. Other economic factors contributed to this.

A key issue was the reordering of Britain's trade and investment patterns. In 1950, the proportion of British exports going to the Commonwealth stood at 47.7 per cent. Despite preferential tariffs, by 1960 this had fallen to 40.2 per cent. There was a comparable decline in imports from the Commonwealth from 41.9 per cent of Britain's total in 1950 to 34.6 per cent in 1960. In addition to this, it was clear that the British manufacturing industry lacked competitiveness in terms of price and quality. Britain's share of world trade continued to decline and competition from West Germany and Japan was damaging. A similar pattern emerged with private investment in colonial development. City investors became increasingly reluctant to enter the sterling area. The colonies were becoming increasingly irrelevant to Britain's economic needs and so there was no sound economic reason to maintain them. The issue was not merely a question of the costs of maintaining the colonies; it was primarily a pragmatic matter. The colonies were simply not delivering the economic cushion that Britain needed.

Macmillan's cost-benefit analysis

As Anthony Eden's Chancellor, Macmillan had tried to cut colonial development aid. As the new Prime Minister in 1957, he asked the Cabinet's Colonial Policy Committee for 'something like a profit and loss account for each of our colonial possessions'. This was to be done in order to calculate 'the balance of advantage...of losing or keeping each particular territory'. As T. Hopkins notes in *Macmillan's Audit of Empire, 1957* (1997), this audit convinced Macmillan that dismantling the British Empire would not damage Britain's economic interests. David Reynolds, in *Britannia Overruled* (1991), makes an incisive comment when he notes that 'economic benefit was no longer a positive reason for maintaining formal control, as in the heyday of the sterling area in the decade after the war...It did not dictate decolonisation'. At the heart of Macmillan's cost-benefit analysis lies the fact that Britain was no longer benefiting from an empire and therefore the primary objective in British post-war colonialism, from an economic perspective, had not been achieved. It was not so much that the empire was costing Britain too much to run, but rather that the profits from the enterprise were simply not worth the effort. This was reinforced by the shift in Britain's economic priorities in a developing European and world economic structure. Thus economic factors played a passive rather than an active role in promoting decolonisation. Decolonisation was not the direct outcome of purely economic considerations.

Macmillan was the catalyst who triggered a more rapid pace of decolonisation, but, from an economic point of view, it was the Second World War that acted as the key turning point. What the war did was to focus Britain's colonial priorities. The priority became economic opportunism and the economic exploitation of colonies. When that failed, then decolonisation followed. The economic crisis left by war created a new economic pragmatism towards colonialism and it was Macmillan who guided British policy through this change.

Britain's growing interest in the EEC

With the creation of the EEC in 1957, Europe rapidly became the focal point of British economic interests. As the EEC strengthened European economies, Britain became a major trader with continental Europe. Between 1954 and 1960, Britain's exports to Europe rose by 29 per cent compared to a one per cent increase with the sterling area countries. Once again, it was economic interests that acted as a primary motive in British policy towards Europe. If the colonies could not provide the economic opportunities that Britain needed, then Europe might. In effect, British trading orientation moved away from a colonial base towards a European focus. The Commonwealth was becoming increasingly less relevant to Britain's economic priorities. This change was partly due to the shift in trading partners to be found amongst Commonwealth states. Australia and New Zealand, for example, were becoming increasingly interested in the economic development of the Pacific Rim and South East Asia.

CONCLUSIONS

Between 1870 and 1980 there were three distinct phases in terms of economic factors influencing imperial expansion and decolonisation. The period between 1870 and 1914 suggests that economic factors, although relevant to imperial expansion, played a relatively limited role in determining the expansion. Government policy was influenced by economic pressures, but there were other, more significant, factors that drove expansionism. Economic influences were directed towards areas of the empire that were perceived as profitable.

The period 1919 to the outbreak of the Second World War suggests a growing dependency upon imperial trade because of the economic impact of the First World War and the collapse of the world economy. This period was not characterised by increased British control in order to establish economic advantage, but by a real sense of cooperation between Britain and the Dominions. Again, it is true to say that other non-economic factors laid the foundations for significant changes after 1945.

The post-Second World War era was one in which economic pragmatism drove British policy. Decolonisation was certainly facilitated, if not initiated, by Britain's changed economic priorities in its relationship with the empire. The economic advantages of empire were outweighed by the costs. This realisation, and the changed emphasis in perceived British interests through a desire for closer economic ties with the USA and Europe, certainly accelerated the momentum towards decolonisation.

SECTION 3

How significant were international relations in the rise and fall of Britain's empire?

Britain's rise as an imperial power was not significantly determined by international issues. The empire did offer strategic opportunities on a global scale but there was no concerted plan to develop Britain's global role in any structured way. Until about 1870, Britain was committed to a European balance of power and imperialism was primarily an economic activity. Nevertheless, by 1900, imperial power had become an indicator of great power status. Britain's empire was a measure of its international power. The relationship Britain developed with the empire during the twentieth century did rest on how the empire could be used to promote at least the image of unity under Great Britain and at best to contribute towards protecting Britain at times of crisis. The latter position becomes particularly significant from 1939.

STRATEGIC ISSUES BEFORE 1914

Africa

The classic example of imperialist expansionism came in Africa in the last quarter of the nineteenth century. In 1891, the Prime Minister, Lord Salisbury, commented on this expansionism: 'I do not exactly know the cause of this sudden revolution, but there it is'. Salisbury may have been uncertain but later historians have been less reticent than him to offer their interpretations. Much of the historiography of this 'scramble for Africa' has focused on international relations theories. In 1954, A.J.P. Taylor produced his work *The Struggle for Mastery in Europe*. In this he argued that British imperial expansionism in Africa was the direct result of shifts that had taken place in European power politics. From the 1870s, the European balance of power had become less certain, particularly with the rise of a united Germany. Taylor linked this process to the rise in aggressive European nationalism, which led directly to overseas expansionism in order to confirm international status amongst European states, particularly Germany. In his mind, the partition of Africa was an unplanned and spontaneous process, but it occurred because of increasing European rivalry before 1914.

This notion of an unplanned reaction to European rivalries is also emphasised by R. Robinson and J. Gallagher in their 1961 work, *Africa and the Victorians: The Official Mind of Imperialism*. Their view is that Britain's preferred policy was one of no expansion, but this was untenable in view of the expansionism of Germany and France. From this point, the scramble becomes uncontrollable until the entire continent of Africa has been absorbed as part of European empires. They develop the argument by suggesting that Egypt and the Suez Canal were of central importance to Britain's empire, particularly India. Britain's control of Egypt and the canal stimulated a response from its rivals, which Britain had in turn to react to. As Robinson and Gallagher comment: 'From start to finish, the partition of tropical Africa was driven by the persistent crisis in Egypt. When the British entered Egypt on their own, the scramble began.'

A wider interpretation of the impact of international relations is proffered by Paul Kennedy in *The Rise and Fall of the Great Powers* (1988). Essentially, Kennedy's argument is based on the view that other European states wanted to establish great power status by imperialism. Britain responded to this by expanding its own empire through Africa in order to maintain a level of imperial dominance over its European rivals.

A balanced analysis of the growth of the British Empire in Africa may suggest that Britain's actions were initially driven by protective rather than expansive motives. Before Britain's involvement with the Suez Canal, its priority was to protect its commercial interests in West and South Africa. The threat to free trade in West Africa was posed by the French and it revealed that Britain's trading supremacy was no longer absolute. Rather than opening doors for new free trade opportunities, Britain's European commercial rivals were closing them though protectionist control in the areas they occupied. The defence of the new Suez Canal became a fundamental issue in British imperial policy. The canal was the route to India, the 'jewel' in Britain's imperial crown. The canal was the strategic focal point in the defence of India and Britain's commercial and strategic interests there. The hinterlands of Africa assumed major strategic importance in Britain's quest to protect the commercial route to India. The canal was also of supreme strategic importance in the protection of India. The protection of what Britain already had, rather than a determination to acquire more, was the main determinant in British expansionism. The need to protect existing British interests arose from the commercial and strategic threats implied in the imperialism of other western European states.

The second Boer War, 1899

Britain's willingness to go to war in South Africa at the end of the 'scramble' also reveals the impact of international relations on imperial policy. The British High Commissioner for South Africa, Alfred Milner, showed this when he said that there was a 'greater issue than the grievances of the uitlanders at stake…our supremacy in South Africa…and our existence as a great power in the world is involved'.

The war had very significant consequences for Britain's interpretation of how its international status should be protected and what relationship this would have with imperialism. The decade prior to the war had been dominated by a commitment to pursue an independent foreign policy that was not dependent upon foreign alliances. This policy of 'splendid isolation' highlighted Britain's confidence in its international status. The Boer War ended that policy and a series of diplomatic agreements with Japan, Russia and France quickly followed. The notion that Britain could maintain its power by a form of dependency upon its empire had been lost through the war. International relations and the rapid growth of other European power bases, particularly Germany, now demanded that international alliances rather than pure imperialism directed Britain's immediate future planning. Despite this, the empire remained central to Britain's power base, even after the First World War.

THE INTERWAR YEARS, 1919–39

Britain's great power status in 1919 was intact but seriously weakened. The interwar years illustrated a significant shift in Britain's perception of how its empire could contribute to its international status. In many ways, Britain's imperial strategy involved projecting the idea of imperial unity in order to promote the image of Britain's global power base. This is well illustrated in the attempts Britain made to accommodate the demands for greater independence from the Dominion states.

In terms of international relations, this period revealed the empire to be a liability rather than an asset. The empire needed to be defended but Britain's economic resources were so undermined by the war that defence was intolerably expensive. The empire became a source of continuous political problems. The demands of Indian nationalists reinforced the problems. Despite these issues, Britain's strategy was never to simply abandon its empire as an irrelevancy. In the pre-Second World War period, empire was losing its significance as a measure of international status. The outbreak of war in 1939 represented the last great show of apparent imperial unity against a common enemy. The war simply accelerated a process of imperial decline that had already begun in 1919. However, it was in the post-war world that Britain once again attempted to use its empire as a major tool in enhancing its international status.

BRITAIN, THE USA, AND THE COLD WAR

Britain and the quest for global power, 1945–56

In 1945, Britain was determined to avoid becoming merely a regional European power. The empire was perceived as having a key role to play in protecting and enhancing Britain's status as a global power. Britain's aspirations of developing its international power were central to the development of British imperial policy. Foreign and imperial policy complimented each other. As Ernest Bevin commented in January 1948 in a Cabinet memorandum:

> *Backed by the power and resources of the Commonwealth and of the Americas, it should be possible to develop our own power and influence to equal that of the USA and the USSR. We have the material resources in the colonial empire, if we develop them…we should be able to carry out our task in a way which will show clearly that we are not subservient to the USA or to the Soviet Union.*

Even by 1949, when it was clear that Britain needed a close alliance with the USA, the empire was still regarded as an essential component in preventing complete subservience to the USA. In essence, Britain's determination to retain as much of the empire as it could was part of an international strategic plan to preserve global influence. The retention of the empire at this point was primarily a means devised to achieve that end rather than an end in itself. Clearly some areas of the empire were more significant contributors to this strategy than were others.

The Middle East

This was certainly a region of strategic and economic importance to Britain. The Middle East was largely part of Britain's 'informal' empire. The impetus underlying Britain's determination to retain the Middle East came partly from the economic importance of secure oil supplies, but also from strategic factors. Any withdrawal could enable Russia to assume greater influence in the region. Britain needed to preserve its imperial presence in order to address its Cold War paranoia regarding Russian expansionism. In addition to this, as R.F. Holland notes in his work *The Pursuit of Greatness: Britain and the World Role, 1900–70* (1991), a British presence in the region would strengthen Britain's influence over the USA. The USA's influence in the region had yet to be established and it was primarily for this reason that Britain had an advantage over the USA. Holland comments that the British believed that the region was one where 'the Americans…could be manoeuvred and if necessary blackmailed into following the British wake, rather than vice versa'. In terms of Britain's international status, a presence in the Middle East was crucial.

The Far East

A similar approach to Britain's Far Eastern Empire was adopted. The maintenance of Britain's global power was to be protected through the retention of territories in the Far East. Certainly, the outbreak of war in Korea, especially when communist China intervened in the war, heightened the strategic importance of South East Asia. As the region became one of Cold War confrontation, it became essential for Britain's international status to have a power base in the region in order to resist the spread of communism. Once again, the end was to preserve British global influence by stemming the spread of communism. The empire was a vital tool in the fulfilment of this objective. Britain asserted its anti-communist credentials when it used extensive force to stop a communist nationalist uprising in Malaya.

The impact of the Cold War

W. R. Louis and R. Robinson make a telling observation in their work *The Imperialism of Decolonisation* (1994) when they comment on the significance of the Cold War as a positive factor for British post-war imperialism: 'competition between the two superpowers came to the rescue of the empire'. From 1947, the overriding priority in the USA's international objectives was the containment of communism and of Soviet expansionism, as defined through the Truman Doctrine. Ideologically, the USA was committed to decolonisation, but in terms of the protection of its vital national interests, British imperialism was a marked asset in Britain as an ally. However, this apparent US pro-imperialism was a purely pragmatic stance taken in the early Cold War period. Arab nationalism was a significant factor in determining the direction of US Middle Eastern policy. By 1956, it was clear to the USA that Nasser was a more potent force in terms of containing the spread of communism in the Middle East than was the maintenance of a British presence there. US pressure forced Britain to withdraw from Suez and this clearly indicated that, in terms of US interests in the Middle East, Nasser was more significant than Britain. This was to prove particularly important when Nasser took control of the canal in 1956. US thinking in terms of anti-colonialism was very much determined by Cold War priorities and this is well illustrated through the work of M. Kahler in his study *The United States and the Third World* (1990). In this he comments that the US proved:

> *very selective in its choice of nationalist clients in the Third World...Even in the absence of open communist support, radical nationalists were often suspected of communist leanings; they were perceived as...serving the interests of communism by creating instability and aligning themselves with the Soviet Union.*

US anti-colonialism was restrained by and based on pure pragmatism. The USA exerted some pressure on Britain to decolonise, but this was always within the context of the USA's Cold War interests. There was relatively little pressure brought to bear in Africa because there were no real Cold War interests at stake there. However, an interesting example of US pressure on Britain may be viewed through the incidents in Iran in 1951.

Britain controlled much of the Iranian oil industry when, in 1951, its interests were nationalised by the Iranians. The USA prevented any British military action against Iran because they feared a Russian attack in northern Iran, the subsequent destabilisation of the Middle East, and the expansion of Soviet influence in the region. Nicholas White, in his work *Decolonisation: The British Experience since 1945*, offers some useful analytical observations on the influence of the USA on Britain's decision to accelerate decolonisation from the early 1960s when he comments that, 'Nor was the empire always dismantled by a cosy Anglo–American "coalition". The "special relationship" was often transitory.' A real test of the 'special relationship' came in 1956 with the outbreak of the Suez Canal Crisis.

SUEZ: A TURNING POINT?

The British and French constructed a plan to remove Nasser and this was refined at Sevres. The French, British and Israelis determined that Israel would attack Egypt on 29 October. This would be followed by an Anglo–French ultimatum to Egypt and Israel to end the war. The next step was to be the introduction of an Anglo–French force with the role of restoring peace in the Middle East. The actual task was to remove Nasser and restore French and British control over the canal, and with it British and French influence in Egypt and the Middle East.

The USA, the Soviet Union, a number of independent Commonwealth countries and the Arab states of the Middle East condemned the action. The US Vice-President, Richard Nixon, commented poignantly on the USA's position when he said:

> For the first time in history, we have shown independence of Anglo–French policies towards Asia and Africa, which seemed to us to reflect the colonial tradition. That declaration of independence has had an electrifying effect throughout the world.

What matters here is not an analysis of US policy but the impact this decision had on Britain in terms of its colonial policy. Anthony Eden's priority during the Suez Crisis was to secure Middle Eastern oil supplies to Britain and maintain Britain's imperial prestige.

The affair triggered a financial crisis for Britain and it starkly revealed the economic influence the USA held over Britain. As Kunz notes in *The Importance of Having Money: The Economic Diplomacy of the Suez Crisis* (1989), 'The question became not whether, but when, Britain would bow to American imperatives.' Macmillan, as Chancellor of the Exchequer in November 1956, reinforced this view of US influence when he commented that US 'good will could not be obtained without an immediate and unconditional undertaking to withdraw the Anglo–French force from Port Said'. The prospect of a financial collapse with no support coming from the USA left Eden no choice other than to unconditionally withdraw from Suez which he did.

Britain attempted to present its actions over the Suez Crisis as those carried out by a state sensitive to UN thinking. Britain and France suggested that they had acted positively to restore peace between Egypt and the Israelis and this was in no sense an act of aggression by them against the Egyptians. Few in the international community took this excuse seriously. The UN sent in a peacekeeping force to administer the peaceful withdrawal of Israeli forces. Britain was not part of this force.

To what extent was the Suez Crisis important for British imperial policy?

The historiography of the Suez Crisis is clearly divided as to whether the crisis was profoundly significant or largely irrelevant to Britain's colonial policy. Some historians regard the crisis as a watershed, while others view it as an overrated incident whose consequences have been exaggerated in terms of its contribution to post-war decolonisation.

A turning point?

R.F. Holland, in his work *European Decolonisation, 1918–81: An Introductory Survey* (1985), argues that the Suez Crisis enabled the USA to influence British politics by exploiting the crisis in order to engineer the resignation of Anthony Eden. The new Prime Minister, Harold Macmillan, was popular with the US administration because he was compliant with US anti-colonialism. In effect, the Suez Crisis brought into office the arch-decoloniser, Macmillan. The fact the crisis led to Macmillan's appointment is accurate but it does not, in itself, suggest that the Suez Crisis was significant in accelerating British decolonisation. Any other political setback could have equally well led to the end of Eden's Premiership.

A more direct analysis is offered by Lapping in his article *Did Suez Hasten the End of Empire?* (1987). He argues that 'Suez…is the single most significant initiative by the main imperial powers that speeded up the end of empire process…Everybody saw that the imperial gunboat no longer worked'. Lapping goes on to conclude that 'Macmillan and Macleod changed policy because they saw that, in the light of all the changes speeded up by Suez, they had no choice'. Essentially, the crisis revealed Britain's inability, in terms of foreign policy, to function independently of the USA. Suez laid bare Britain's limited ability to function as an imperial power in the post-war world. Lapping also argues that Nasser not only turned away from the West after the crisis, but he also offered support to African nationalist movements. This heightened the anti-colonial pressure on Britain that was increasing throughout Africa, and it encouraged the USA to take a more proactive interest in African colonial developments. In *Eclipse of Empire* (1991), Low sums up the significance of Suez when he comments that 'the British Cabinet lost its collective nerve after Suez and decided to climb out of any situations that might involve them in critical episodes overseas'.

Much of the historiography focuses on the centrality of Britain's relationship, and dependency upon, the USA. W.R. Louis and R. Robinson, in their work *The Imperialism of Decolonisation* (1994), argue a strong case to suggest the importance of the Anglo–American relationship in influencing British imperial policy in the context of the Cold War. This view is made abundantly clear through the author's comment that 'Once and for all, it was established that Britain had to work in concert with the USA…Suez exposed the US essentials underlying British imperial power for all to see'.

An event of limited importance?

The Suez Crisis was an event that concerned the imperial status of Britain. It did trigger a financial crisis and it did spotlight a potential conflict within Britain's relationship with its closest and most important ally, the USA. Despite this, how significant was the crisis in accelerating the moves towards decolonisation?

The long-term impact of Suez has been challenged. In Africa, Nicholas White suggests in his work *Decolonisation: The British Experience Since 1945* (1999), 'The outcome of Suez neither inspired nationalist leaders nor frightened colonial administrations.' Britain was influenced much more directly by the determination of widespread African nationalism than by the impact of Suez. Low argues that the process of nationalism was not determined by the outcomes of Suez. African nationalism pre-dated Suez and it was African nationalism that directly influenced Macmillan's decision to accept African decolonisation.

The idea of significant issues pre-dating the Suez Crisis is also developed by Porter and Stockwell in their work *British Imperial Policy and Decolonisation, 1938–64* (1989). They suggest that domestic priorities had greater significance in contributing to decolonisation than did Suez. The empire was expensive and economically unproductive compared to other forms of financial investment. Economically, it was clear before 1956 that colonial economic development was not working. Porter and Stockwell take the view that, politically as well as economically, the empire was a liability rather than an asset. Suez did not establish this reality; it already existed. What the crisis did do was underline the economic realities that Britain was already aware of. Suez made Britain more aware of the vulnerability of sterling.

Suez did not bring about a major British foreign policy review. Britain's relationship with the USA remained intact and this was most clearly illustrated in the Anglo–American cooperation to prevent Egypt's influence extending into Jordan and the Lebanon. Further Anglo–American unity was shown as joint forces landed in the Lebanon and Jordan immediately following the Iraq Revolution in 1958 that brought the pro-British regime there to an end. Britain's role in the Middle East after Suez diminished but nevertheless continued to exist. Britain retained considerable interests in Jordan, Cyprus, Aden and the Persian Gulf.

As a postscript, it should be noted that to suggest that the USA was anti-imperialist would be to misrepresent the nature of US national interests. Ideologically, the USA opposed empire, but in terms of international relations within a Cold War context, the USA was deeply sensitive to the possibility of newly independent Third World states falling into the hands of the communists or under the influence of the Soviet Union. The USA did not have a simplistic decolonisation policy that it unreservedly imposed on Britain in return for its economic and military support. Hence, although Britain had a 'special relationship' with the USA, that did not translate into the USA determining British imperial policy. What did matter to both Britain and the USA was that resistance to nationalism could force nationalist groups into the arms of the communists. Therefore, 'friendly' nationalist groups could be accommodated.

CONCLUSIONS

The 'scramble for Africa' clearly illustrates the importance of international relations in imperial expansionism. However, the expansion should be viewed as an essential reaction to the expansionism of other states rather than Britain seeing imperial expansionism as a necessary indicator of global power. There was no defined intention to act as a global power or indeed to seek to become one. After 1945, the empire is most clearly used as a tool to enhance Britain's international status and bargaining power in the new reality of a bi-polar world. To this extent, a significant shift had taken place in terms of how Britain perceived its empire. In many respects, the empire, even though Britain's hold on it had dramatically diminished, became much more relevant to Britain's international status after 1945 than it had been before then.

To what extent did Britain's perception of its empire change over time?

Even before the First World War, Britain's ability to retain its empire fully intact was in serious doubt. The empire was a disparate group of states at completely different stages of economic and social development. Britain never lost sight of the advantages of empire, nor did it cling on to empire when the cost was greater than the benefit. Throughout the twentieth century, successive governments compromised their authority for the greater good of British interests. British imperial policy was driven primarily by pragmatism rather than blind fanaticism.

POPULAR IMPERIALISM IN THE 1880s AND 1890s

Gladstone and the empire

During the Midlothian Campaign, which led to electoral victory in 1880, Gladstone revealed his lack of support for imperialism. He condemned Disraeli for encouraging the British public to display a 'lust for glory, aggressiveness, and chauvinism'. Gladstone's imperial position was not fully backed within his own party and certainly not backed by the Conservatives. The Liberal Party was made up of a wide range of factions and political views. One of its leading members, Sir William Harcourt, described it as 'like the kingdom of heaven, the Liberal Party is a house of many mansions'. Within the party were a powerful group of Liberal imperialists. An example of the influence of this group lies in the actions of one of its leading figures, Lord Rosebery, in 1893. Rosebery gathered Cabinet support against Gladstone for the reinforcement of military power in Egypt. Rosebery also secured control of Uganda as part of the strategic defences of Egypt despite Gladstone's vehement opposition.

Despite Gladstone's victory in 1880, and his lukewarm imperialism, there was plenty of popular support for imperialism. In the mid-1880s, jingoistic imperialism was at its height within the popular mentality. The general public was bombarded with media controlled images that eulogised the virtues of imperialism. A classic example of how Gladstone's perception of the relationship Britain should have with its empire and how this was grossly at variance with the apparent popular perception is illustrated through the fall of Khartoum in 1885.

A cartoon depicting Gladstone as a humiliated lion published in 1885

PEACE WITH DISHONOUR

"THE WILD MOB'S MILLION FEET, WILL KICK YOU FROM YOUR PLACE —
BUT THEN — TOO LATE, TOO LATE" *Tennyson.*

Grief and anger swept the nation. Queen Victoria sent Gladstone a telegram, which read: 'These news from Khartoum are frightful, and to think that all this might have been prevented and many precious lives saved by earlier action is too fearful.' Gladstone was unrepentant and part of his reply to the Queen read: 'Mr Gladstone does not presume to estimate the means of judgement possessed by Your Majesty, but so far as his information goes, he is not altogether able to follow the conclusion which Your Majesty has been pleased thus to announce to him.'

Punch published an illustration depicting a distraught Britannia. It is important to note that Gladstone saw the empire as a trading empire and accepted it through a vision of a federation of self-governing states. This perception of Gladstone as an anti-imperialist is developed through the work of Richard Shannon in his work *Crisis of Imperialism* (1977).

Explanations of late nineteenth-century imperialism

The 1880s and 1890s were periods of imperial expansionism, particularly in Africa, but Britain also had a lasting commitment to the rest of its global empire. Historians have attempted to explain why Britain appeared to embrace expansionist imperialism during this period and how the wider empire was rationalised in British imperial thinking. Essentially, there are four main theories as to why Britain adopted a more proactive form of imperialism after 1870.

Social imperialism

This is based on the view that imperialism offered the British ruling classes the means to unite the country behind a popular cause, which would effectively distract Britons from other issues that might threaten the control of the ruling elite. P. Marshall, in *Imperialism* (1990), comments that imperialism was seen as 'a means of uniting…societies behind a great cause and sometimes as a means of heading off working-class discontent'. In this interpretation, the empire is seen as a means of encouraging and instilling a sense of patriotism in the minds of the British people. Patriotism has a dulling effect on the inclination to question and seek social and economic change in Britain and thereby protects the vested interests of the rulers. The Conservative Party cultivated its image as the party of patriotism and, significantly, remained in power for two thirds of the time between 1874 and 1906. It is noteworthy that the success of the Conservatives was not entirely due to popular support for its imperial policies but also due to the decline of the Liberals as political opponents. The promise to control aliens could also keep the working class of the East End of London voting Conservative.

This interpretation implies a type of national obsession with imperialism and patriotism. One of the principle proponents of mass working-class support for imperialism was J.A. Hobson in his work *Imperialism: A Study* (1902). In this he argues:

> *Imperialism is motivated not by the interests of the nation but by those of certain classes who impose the policy of the nation for their own advantage. Imperialism also favours the general cause of Conservatism by diverting public interest and attention away from domestic agitation and the tension it causes in international relations, encourages increased military expenditure, and provides a justification for not implementing social reform.*

This orthodox interpretation of social imperialism has been challenged by subsequent historians.

Revisionist historians such as Richard Price have questioned the orthodox view. Price suggests, in *An Imperial War and the Working Class* (1972), that many working-class men volunteered to fight in the Boer War not from an exaggerated sense of patriotism but primarily for pragmatic reasons. Joining an army seeking recruits was the fastest way of escaping the immediacy of poverty. Henry Pelling, in *Popular Politics in the Late Victorian Age* (1967), rejects the view that because music hall entertainment was profoundly jingoistic it reflected a popular working-class view. McDonough challenges the view that the general election victory of the Conservatives in 1900 was a working-class endorsement of imperialism as expressed through the second Boer War. In *The British Empire, 1815–1914* (1994), he comments:

> *Jingoistic candidates from the Conservative and Liberal parties were rejected in many working-class constituencies. It seems that, among the urban working class in 1900, opposition to Irish Home Rule remained a stronger reason than imperialism for voting Conservative.*

It would be misleading to suggest that the working classes were indifferent to the impact of patriotic propaganda or that they lacked any commitment to crown, country and empire. However, the notion that imperial policy was the outcome of an attempt to brainwash the working classes and distract them from real domestic issues simply lacks substantive evidence. Recent research of the kind referred to above is founded on substantive evidence and objectivity rather than the subjective interpretations of Hobson, giving recent interpretations credibility.

Cultural imperialism

This interpretation is founded on altruism. It argues that the expansion of the empire was the outcome of Britain's determination to bring civilisation to uncivilised parts of the world. Implicit in this view is the idea that Britain was convinced of the superiority of its own culture and racial make-up. The concept of social Darwinism served to justify British imperialism, as did the notion that rulers had an obligation to use their superiority and status on behalf of others who were less fortunate. Britain certainly held the view that the cultures of Africans and Asians were primitive and could only benefit from an infusion of British culture.

However, to regard the transfer of culture as a leading factor in the development of imperialism, or indeed, as the driving force behind British 'planning', is to distort the evidence. The extent of the imposition of purely British culture on the colonial masses was very limited. Cultural imperialism did exist. Christian missionaries were sent in large numbers to bring godliness to 'heathen' peoples. However, the primary motive that explains cultural imperialism was that of control. Britain wanted collaborative populations within its colonies. By creating a small, educated group of middle-class natives who benefited from imperialism, Britain could ensure cooperation. These educated elites were conditioned to accept British status and British values. This made control easier. As E. Hobsbawn comments in *The Age of Empire, 1875–1914* (1994), 'Before about 1865, it was possible to see the encounter between British and other cultures in terms of a dialogue. But, by the time of the New Imperialism in the late nineteenth century, the balance had changed. From the 1870s on, African cultures found themselves increasingly unable to resist British penetration.' Cultural imperialism was not a primary end in itself; it was merely a means to an end.

Strategic imperialism

By the late nineteenth century, Britain was facing the emergence of new power bases that appeared to have the capacity to challenge its global power. The European balance of power that had existed since 1815 was, by 1870, far less defined. Germany was a rapidly developing economic force by the 1880s, as was the USA. The expansion of British imperial power in Africa was in part a response to the expansionism of Britain's European rivals. It was also a means of strengthening the protection of routes to India, the 'jewel in the crown', and it enhanced British international prestige. With the concept of a balance of power rapidly being replaced by the notion of territorial expansionism at all costs in Europe, Britain simply could not afford to remain aloof. The scramble for

Africa was very specific to the 1880s and 1890s and in no sense represented the long-term policy route that Britain was fulfilling.

R. Long offers an interesting insight into the nature of imperial expansionism in this period in his work *The Man on the Spot* (1995). In this he notes, 'It was the man on the spot who was a factor in imperial expansion as much as, or sometimes more than, imperial policy which was often opposed to further territory as a matter of policy or on the grounds of expense.' This would suggest that although strategic issues were relevant to expansionism, it often tended to be the result of decisions made at local level rather than the implementation of centrally directed policy. Ad hoc colonialism rather than centralist policy seems to have been characteristic of Britain's late nineteenth-century colonial expansion.

Economic imperialism

The evidence suggests that the importance of economic imperialism has been exaggerated, particularly in the period up to 1914. There was no consistent or concerted policy directed towards economic imperialism. Economic issues were focused on profitability and not every part of the empire was perceived as being profitable.

Thus the end of the nineteenth century witnessed Britain embarking on a phase of imperial expansionism. The period saw the introduction of 'New Imperialism'. Empire became the keystone of Britain's economic and strategic power, although not to the extent that Joseph Chamberlain would have desired. For Chamberlain, the empire was an integral part of Britain's ability to function as an independent great power. For him, it was vital that Britain retained the closest possible economic and strategic links with its empire. Britain was about to enter a new phase of imperialism following the First World War. This was to herald both continuity and change in terms of its relationship with the empire in the context of a changing economic climate and the rise of nationalism within the Dominions and the non-Dominion territories.

THE EMPIRE, 1919–39

One element of continuity in British imperial policy was the determination to preserve the empire. Although the empire had actually grown in size after the First World War due to the dismemberment of the German and Turkish Empires and the creation of mandated territories under the 'temporary' control of the allies, Britain certainly had no further plans for imperial expansionism. The essential priority was to establish a sound economic relationship with the empire and develop it as a British asset rather than a liability.

Trade policy

Throughout the 1920s, Britain continued to pursue the traditional pre-1914 policy of free trade. By 1932, the world had been plunged into an economic depression and in that year imperial preference was introduced to replace free trade. To some extent, this was a reversion to the objectives of Joseph Chamberlain. The control Britain had over the Dominion states was insufficient to exploit the economic opportunities these colonies offered. The Dominions regarded themselves as members of a Commonwealth of countries rather than members of the British Empire. They wanted to sell their goods rather than buy British goods. Nevertheless, Britain exhibited a degree of dependency upon its colonies that had not been apparent at any earlier period.

The Dominions

The white Dominions wanted complete independence from Britain. They wanted the freedom to control not only their own domestic affairs but also their own defence and foreign policies. In 1926, at the Imperial Conference, Britain attempted a damage control exercise in order to retain a semblance of imperial unity. The notion that Britain could assume a high level of control over its Dominions was at an end. Arthur Balfour attempted to define the relationship Britain would have with the Dominions when he stated that they were to be 'united by common allegiance to the crown and freely associated as members of the British Commonwealth of Nations'. Britain's control of part of its empire was declining and the Balfour Declaration of 1926 recognised this but tried to disguise it. The process was furthered in 1931 when the Statute of Westminster confirmed that the Dominions were no longer bound by British laws and that Britain must legally recognise the laws of each Dominion. Britain's grip on this part of its empire was slipping and there was nothing that could be done to prevent it. The priority was to establish a working relationship with the Dominions, which would retain them as allies of Britain and thereby protect Britain's international status.

India

The First World War heightened the demand for greater freedom amongst Indian nationalists. There was no commitment in Britain to a drive towards independence immediately after the war. Gradualism characterised Britain's attitude, but underlying it was the realisation that continuity could not be maintained. As with the Dominions, Britain's basic strategy was to attempt to retain a close relationship but also, in the case of India, to retain as much direct control as possible. On the eve of the end of the war, Edwin Montague, the Secretary of State for India announced that the British government supported 'the increasing association of Indians in every branch of the administration, and the gradual development of self-governing institutions, with a view to the progressive realisation of responsible government in India as an integral part of the British Empire.'

To what extent did Britain's perception of its empire change over time?

The 1919 Government of India Act ensured that the Viceroy retained control of defence and the power to rule by decree. By the late 1920s, British policy was based on conciliation. By 1929, the Viceroy, Lord Irwin, was able to announce that Britain was willing to move towards Dominion status for India. Official British policy was geared to trying to establish a compromise with the nationalists in order to retain some influence in India. Churchill and his few supporters bitterly opposed what they saw as the abandonment of British power in India. Churchill commented:

> We ought to disassociate ourselves in the most public manner from any complicity in the weak…administration of India by the socialists and by the Viceroy acting upon their responsibility. It is alarming to see Mr Gandhi striding half-naked up the steps of the vice-regal palace while he is still organising and conducting a defiant campaign of civil disobedience.

Churchill was already politically marginalized by this point and his views were regarded as irrelevant and outdated.

The 1935 Government of India Act reveals not only a degree of continuity in Britain's desire to retain some influence in India, it also reveals a shift in Britain's perception of its role as an imperial power. This is most effectively shown through the words of Sir Samuel Hoare, the Secretary of State for India. He commented on the Act in 1935:

> I maintain that the old system of paternal government, great as have been its achievements on behalf of the Indian masses in the past, is no longer sufficient. However good it has been, it cannot survive a century of western education, a long period of free speech and our deliberate policy of developing parliamentary government.

The demise of paternalism represented a sea of change in Britain's perception of its role in India.

The Dependencies

These colonies experienced the least shift in the continuity of British colonial thinking. Although some degree of independence may well have been envisaged in the distant future, there was a certainty in the minds of the British colonial masters that these territories needed British protection. The end of paternalism may be heralded in India but it was a long way away as far as the Dependencies were concerned. Alongside this particular aspect of colonial continuity lay the economic reality of continued underdevelopment of the Dependencies by Britain. Between the wars, little changed for the many dependent territories. In many, nationalism was in its embryonic stage and often divided along ethnic lines. Britain could afford to preserve the old order because there was little incentive or need to consider change. The main focus of British interwar imperial policy lay with the Dominions and India.

POST-SECOND WORLD WAR IMPERIAL RELATIONS

The Second World War had had a devastating impact on Britain's economic and strategic status. One of Britain's immediate post-war priorities was to retain as much global influence as possible and protect its economic strength. Both of these objectives were seen as being attainable through the empire. These objectives were certainly not new. If anything, they relate to the late nineteenth century as much as the mid-twentieth century. What had emerged as a result of the war was a greater willingness on Britain's part to recognise the pressure for decolonisation. Even this process was driven by the need to protect British interests rather than the primary focus being on the interests of the states Britain had occupied for generations. The immediate impression of post-war relations with the empire is one of systematic and fairly rapid disengagement and decolonisation. The question is, to what extent is this view accurate? Did Britain simply disengage because its priorities had shifted so dramatically, or was the disengagement more apparent that real?

Economic issues

Throughout most of the 1950s, British policy was based on promoting colonial economic development in order to ensure viable markets for British goods. The policy failed and economic realities turned Britain to more lucrative European and US markets. What changed after 1945 was not Britain's commitment to its empire but the emergence of the realisation that the empire could not deliver the economic advantages it had done before the war. As always, Britain's self-interest remained a paramount factor in determining the relationship it had with its empire.

Despite this apparent shift in British economic thinking, some historians have argued that there was a determination to maintain a degree of economic continuity with the empire. The economic opportunities in imperial trade were still regarded as valuable, even by the late 1950s. Schenk, in her work *Decolonisation and European Economic Integration: The Free Trade Area Negotiations, 1956–8* (1996), refers to a senior Cabinet Minister explaining in 1957 that 'what strengthens the economy of the British Commonwealth must in the long run help to strengthen the economy of Europe; what strengthens the economy of Europe must strengthen the economies of the British Commonwealth.'

The key to British decolonisation and the apparent disengagement strategy was the preservation of post-colonial British 'influence'. At no point was Britain's thinking geared to a complete break. Essentially, Britain wanted all the economic opportunities without the economic costs of empire. This leads to the concept of neo-colonialism. This suggests that although decolonisation took place, disengagement did not. As N. White comments in *Decolonisation: The British Experience Since 1945* (1999), 'It could be argued that western capitalism had evolved to such a point that colonial rule became redundant. Constitutional progress in the colonial empire did not damage Britain's economic interests.' Decolonised states retained capitalist economies and thereby tied themselves into a form of economic dependency upon Britain. The notion that neo-colonialism was a planned process has been challenged by those who argue that the favourable economic outcomes could not have been predicted.

Public opinion

The link between patriotism and imperialism was distinct before 1945. It had declined from its pre-1914 heyday but it was intact. After 1945, there was a major change in the popular attitudes towards imperialism. Although there was a mood of racial superiority still present amongst many Britons, there was also a realisation that British control over other peoples was increasingly becoming anachronistic. This was particularly true after fighting against the Nazi dictatorship during the war. From a purely self-interested viewpoint, many Britons rejected the idea of sending their young men to fight against terrorist nationalist groups in remote colonial hotspots. The British public were no longer driven by jingoist patriotism but by a sense of reconciliation.

Strategic issues

Although the empire appeared to offer a clear strategic advantage to Britain after the war and enabled it to avoid adopting a purely European and regional power base, it was strategic factors that contributed to decolonisation rather the retention of the empire. The Suez Canal disaster convinced Britain that its strategic interests lay in strengthening its influence within the western anti-Soviet alliance system. Increasingly, the problems within the empire were perceived as an unnecessary drain on British military and economic resources. Macmillan's thinking was based on the development of nuclear weapons. Britain's post-war strategic priority, since they no longer had naval bases scattered around the world, was to focus government spending on nuclear technology. The cost of suppressing aggressive colonial nationalism was undermining this primary objective. Britain's strategic reorientation after 1945 meant colonial bases were no longer the most significant part of the new strategy.

In 1957, the Foreign Secretary, Selwyn Lloyd, declared that, 'We should take our place where we now most belong, i.e. in Europe with our immediate neighbours.' This was part of Britain's commitment towards a joint Anglo–European nuclear arms programme. Despite this apparent shift towards Europe, Macmillan's government remained committed to a positive strategic relationship with the empire, or its decolonised successors. As with economic issues, Britain did not perceive decolonisation as a break with the strategic advantages of having an empire. As L.J. Butler states in his work *Winds of Change: Britain, Europe and the Commonwealth, 1959–61* (1993), decolonisation was 'the translation of the colonial relationship into something more palatable in an age of Cold War and mass nationalism, a more flexible system of ties attuned to modern requirements'. Butler's analysis succinctly explains the basis of British thinking in decolonisation. Even though Britain did not retain its empire, it did strive to retain the influence the empire had formerly provided and could still provide in the new context of the Cold War.

The 'wind of change'

This speech was perceived as a profound break with continuity and the final nail in Britain's imperial coffin. Macmillan had broken with Britain's long-standing policy of maintaining a close relationship with the empire. The speech delivered to the South African Parliament in 1960 seemed to be the high point of the new anti-imperialist orthodox thinking. Continuity with the past had ended abruptly.

However, this interpretation of the speech may be challenged. Macmillan was not abandoning the empire. His thinking was directly in line with many of his Conservative predecessors, including Churchill. Macmillan sought to preserve Britain's strategic and economic strengths by exploiting the empire via a different route than the traditional one. The British Empire would transform into the British Commonwealth. As J. Darwin comments, in *The Fear of Falling: British Politics and Imperial Decline Since 1900* (1986), 'decolonisation was the continuation of empire by another means'. Macmillan was no different from many who had gone before him. Britain may not have had the authority, but it still had the influence. Macmillan's pragmatism and his objectives were certainly consistent with those before 1914. The ends had not changed; it was simply the means that had taken a new direction.

CONCLUSIONS

The perceptions of empire amongst Britons had changed over a hundred-year period. Patriotism was no longer in vogue and nor was the validity of having an empire by the 1960s. However, mass support for imperialism was as dubious a concept in 1900 as it was in 1960. The one striking continuity that pervades British imperial policy throughout the period is the determination by Britain to protect its own self-interests. This could be done by using anything from limited and controlled decolonisation through to full-blown decolonisation of the kind that followed the Second World War. Again, there was a remarkable degree of continuity in British objectives. It was the methodology that changed. Economic and strategic priorities remained consistent in their importance throughout the period. Economic advantage was as central to British imperial thinking in 1960 as it had been in 1900.

How valid is the view that colonial nationalism was the key to decolonisation?

Nationalism undoubtedly contributed to independence, but its impact was variable across the British Empire. At times it was the direct causal link of independence, while on other occasions it was a factor amongst many others. There was no concept of nationalism that permeated the empire. Often, nationalist groups were in conflict with rival nationalist groups. Perhaps the one common thread that did run through nationalist movements was the determination to preserve national ethnic character and cultural identity. Economic independence and opportunity was a further important issue that drove nationalist thinking.

THE DEVELOPMENT OF COLONIAL NATIONALISM

The contribution of nationalism towards decolonisation was not simply a post-1945 phenomenon. Nationalism was a long-term process, which had its origins rooted well before 1945. The historiography of the origins of nationalism suggests a varied range of priorities that led to the decolonisation of post-1945. The historiography attempts to establish an analysis of the interaction between the imperial ruler, Britain, and the ruled, the colonial subjects. One predominant theme is that of the long-term continuity of anti-colonial resistance and opposition dating back to the early points in colonial rule. Such an approach has been developed by A. Boahen in his work *African Perspectives on Colonialism* (1989). A similar analysis was used by T. Ranger in *African Reactions to the Imposition of Colonial Rule in East and Central Africa* (1969). These views are based on an intentionalist analysis that suggests a long-term and planned process of resistance to colonial rule by indigenous populations.

A more structuralist analysis has been presented by R. Robinson in his work *Non-European Foundations of European Imperialism: Sketch for a Theory of Collaboration* (1972). In this, Robinson argues that British colonial power rested on collaboration with indigenous elites. By the middle of the twentieth century, this pool of collaborative elites had declined to a point where colonial rule came to its inevitable conclusion. In effect, colonial rule was no longer viable because native collaboration had evaporated. This dependency theory is also promoted by J. Gallagher through his work *The Decline, Revival and Fall of the British Empire* (1982). An elaboration of the structuralist approach is presented by D. Low in his work *Eclipse of Empire* (1991). In this, the analysis does not turn on the importance of collaborators and the subsequent decline but on the idea that British power was founded upon its willingness to appease the rich peasants through the economic advantage they perceived in imperialism. While imperialism held positive economic outcomes for this group, it could survive. Low argues that Britain increasingly moved away from this priority and consequently lost control of its colonies.

Nationalism may be seen as an inevitable outcome of the changes that colonialism brought to the societies it sought to control. For example, in Africa, British colonies experienced a process of rapid urbanisation. New economic practices were rapidly introduced, particularly in agriculture. The outcome was the resurgence of a demand to protect ethnic and cultural identity. In Africa, this became a central factor amongst nationalist leaders. Colonialism also brought with it educational opportunities through the Christian missions, for example. This, combined with the economic developments, enabled a small but articulate middle class to emerge and thus formed the foundation of much anti-colonialism.

By the late 1930s, many young Africans were going abroad for a European-style education. This was perceived as crucial to establishing freedom. Many, such as Jomo Kenyatta, went to the London School of Economics where Harold Laski taught left-wing political science and where they were able to meet anti-empire politicians within the British Labour Party. The basic problem for pre-war nationalist figures in Africa, and indeed in South East Asia, was that many of the ideas were experienced only by the urban elites and did not often penetrate into the rural hinterlands. A further problem for African nationalism lay in the deep divisions that often existed between competing groups. This is particularly well illustrated in Kenya. Anti-colonial options ranged from protecting cultural, ethnic and tribal identity to achieving territorial independence through to full blown Pan-Africanism.

Nationalism was a particularly difficult process to develop in countries that had a significant range of ethnic and cultural differences. In India, there was a major religious division between Hindus and Muslims. This was compounded even further by regionalism. Between the wars, nationalist fervour in India had been predominantly Hindu inspired. Gandhi's personal charisma placed him at the head of Indian nationalism and the Congress Party. The origins of the Congress Party dated back to 1885. By the turn of the twentieth century, the Congress Party was beginning to adopt a more proactive approach towards independence. India was a classic example of nationalist agitation after the First World War, during the 1930s, and during the Second World War, being effective in influencing British imperial thinking but also illustrating the vast divisions between nationalist groups. For the Muslims, an independent India meant a Hindu ruled India and this they could not accept.

Religious-based inter-communal conflict seriously undermined nationalist strength in India before the Second World War. These religious divisions were added to the regionalism that characterised the Indian sub-continent. As F. McDonough comments in *The British Empire, 1815–1914* (1994), 'These deep regional differences in Indian society would have to be overcome if nationalism was to stand any chance of winning widespread support.' For Britain, India was the 'jewel in the crown' and there was no commitment towards offering independence, certainly not before the Second World War. The barriers impeding the growth of Indian nationalism were significantly greater than the benefits of nationalism. There was no doubt that nationalism in India was divided, but this did not necessarily mean that it was weakened. In 1935, Muhammed Ali Jinnah revitalised the Muslim League group by ruthlessly exploiting Muslim fears of Hindus in order to unite Muslims into a cohesive force. The primary issue for Indian nationalists before 1945 was not whether independence would happen but what form it would take.

The development of nationalist opposition to Britain was uneven across the empire.

THE SECOND BOER WAR, 1899–1902

The first significant expression of anti-British nationalism came at the very end of the nineteenth century in the form of the Boer War. Essentially, the war was the outcome of aggressive British imperialism in South Africa and Britain's 'victory' proved that such an attitude would not work. Britain won the military campaigns but it failed to establish any lasting legitimacy for militarism as a means of controlling imperial possessions. The war made a major contribution to the transformation of British attitudes towards empire and to the rejection of Chamberlain's vision of imperialism. It also reinforced the perception that Britain's ability to maintain an empire by force was simply not certain. The issue of 'national efficiency' that followed the war was most obviously displayed through the liberal reforms from 1906. Another outcome was the realisation by Britain that nationalists could, and would, make very effective attempts to defend their status and ethnic identity.

In their work *Africa and the Victorians: The Official Mind of Imperialism* (1961), R. Robinson and J. Gallagher argue that the war was a response to Afrikaner nationalism and the threat it posed to British interests in South Africa. Britain's support for the uitlanders was part of a strategy to counter balance the power of the Boers and create the 'collaborator' population that was so central to preserving British imperial influence. Britain had to confront Boer nationalism in order to maintain the framework of control upon which the empire was founded. Victory in the war was taken as evidence that the strategy of developing and protecting a collaborator population was the correct strategy to preserve the empire as cheaply and as efficiently as possible.

In his work *The Origins of the South African War: Joseph Chamberlain and the Diplomacy of Imperialism, 1895–9* (1980), A.N. Porter argues that the war was an act of aggressive imperialism in which the interests of the uitlanders were merely used as a pretext to gain popular support for the war in Britain. Chamberlain summed up the real British motive when he commented in the House of Commons, 'What is now at stake is the position of Great Britain in South Africa – and with it the estimate formed of our power and influence in our colonies and throughout the world.' What Chamberlain was attempting to establish was the centrality of South Africa to Britain's imperial image. Britain could not allow a fledgling nation of Dutch expatriots to establish its influence in an area Britain regarded as its power base. The irony of the Boer War was that the Boers received Home Rule in 1906 and the Union of South Africa was recognised in 1910. Nationalism had not been defeated and this was to prove to be a significant reality for other embryonic nationalist groups in other parts of the British Empire.

INDIAN NATIONALISM

In 1935, Britain had already conceded that India would eventually attain Dominion status. By 1937, the prominent nationalist party, the Indian National Congress, held a majority in the Indian provinces. On 6 July 1942, Gandhi announced the 'Quit India' campaign and called upon the British to 'purify themselves by surrendering power in India'. He told the All-India Congress Committee, 'We shall either free India or die in the attempt.' A period of intense violence followed and there were mass arrests of All-India nationalists, which effectively removed Congress as a nationalist force at that point in time. The campaign had shown that mass opposition could make India almost ungovernable. This was a particularly damaging reality when Britain was facing an increasingly serious threat in the Far East from Japanese military advances towards India. The fall of Malaya reinforced what was becoming a reality, that the British were in no position to prevent Indian independence.

The great irony in India was not that nationalism was ineffective in bringing about independence but that the conflicting national groups delayed independence. Attlee's post-war Labour government wanted a united India based upon a federal structure. This was the best way to ensure Britain's access to strategic military bases and airfields would be secured. Stafford Cripps' 1946 proposal for an Indian federation that would have responsibility for foreign policy, defence, communications and finance was rejected by the Muslim League because of its fears of a Congress-dominated centre. Serious rioting followed and the League was uncompromising in its determination to establish a separate and independent state of Pakistan. Britain decided to withdraw from India regardless of any agreement between Congress and the League.

By 1947, British rule in India had collapsed. The primary issue was not about the attainment of independence: it was about the nature of the structure of an independent Indian sub-continent. The initiatives lay with the nationalists, as Wavell commented in December 1946, 'We have lost nearly all power to control events.' It was not the Second World War that acted as the decisive turning point in the achievement of independence. That was already an unofficial reality before the war started. The First World War was a significant turning point in that it strengthened the determination of Indian nationalists to press Britain for independence at a time of economic crisis in Britain in the interwar years. The key players in Indian nationalism, Gandhi and Jinnah, had displayed an irresistible determination. Indian nationalism was a truly mass movement and one that was driven by religious and ethnic commitment. Had Britain decided that India was an asset, it is highly unlikely that it could have resisted the tremendous force of nationalism there. The Indian experience was one in which nationalism really did override all other factors that contributed in other parts of the British Empire to the granting of independence.

AFRICAN NATIONALISM

Kenya

In *Decolonisation and Independence in Kenya, 1940–93* (1995), W. Maloba comments:

> A *successful national liberation movement thrives on massive national political mobilisation, on adopting a realistic revolutionary theory, but above all on having an ideology of liberation which aims to give its supporters peace, development, dignity and independence. The vision of successful liberation movements in Africa has been egalitarian, non-racist and vehemently opposed to exploitation.*

The Mau Mau

In 1952, the self-styled Kenyan liberation movement, the Mau Mau, began its rebellion against colonial rule. Its membership was almost exclusively from the Kikuyu tribe and consisted largely of disaffected groups who rejected the economic constraints of colonial rule. After the Second World War, changes in agricultural methods were imposed by

Britain in its quest for colonial economic development. There were mass expulsions of Kikuyu squatters in the Rift Valley estates and the recruitment of non-Kikuyu labour by white farmers. These rural issues were exacerbated by urban unemployment and housing shortages. Kikuyu who had rejected rural poverty found themselves trapped in urban poverty. In post-war Kenya, the Mau Mau attracted many young Kikuyu whose economic opportunities had been undermined by colonialism. As David Birmingham writes in *Decolonisation in Africa* (1995), 'The roots of the Kenyan revolution…have to be sought in frustrated success rather than in persistent poverty.'

Mau Mau methods were based on subversion and terror, forms of nationalist action which were certainly not unfamiliar to the British. The questions that need to be considered at this point are can the Mau Mau be seen as a truly nationalist movement and to what extent did its existence contribute to Kenyan independence? The Mau Mau never galvanised popular mass nationalism against British colonial rule. In many respects, Mau Mau actions simply created a civil war in Kenya. Not only did the Mau Mau fight the colonial state, it also fought other Kenyans, particularly the loyalist Agikuyu people. The Mau Mau was never truly representative of the Kenyan people but it was broadly representative of the Kikuyu tribe. A further indicator of the Mau Mau's lack of nationalist credentials lies in the view that political independence, a primary objective of all nationalist movements, was directly linked to cultural freedom and a reassertion of national cultural identity. As H.S. Wilson comments in *African Decolonisation* (1994), 'The politics of nationalism, infused with traditional symbolism and idiom, fiercely defended indigenous society against alien encroachment.' Essentially, Mau Mau nationalism was an expression of Kikuyu economic, political and cultural interests. Although viewed as narrow, Mau Mau nationalism did act as an important catalyst in Kenya's struggle for independence.

The drive towards independence

Mau Mau terrorism exacted an economic cost to Britain. The state of emergency declared in 1952 forced Britain to increase its military commitment in Kenya. More significantly, Britain faced a political price because of Mau Mau tactics. The military occupation of Kenya could not last indefinitely. Equally, Kenya could not return to the pre-emergency position. Some element of reform became essential because of Mau Mau actions. The causal link between reform and the Mau Mau lay in the realisation by the colonial regime that it had to widen the scale of collaboration amongst Kenyans in order to marginalize the Mau Mau and prevent them from being seen as freedom fighters. At this stage, Britain had no specific plan to consider independence for Kenya in the short term.

In effect, black Africans had to be offered increased political and economic opportunities within colonial society to enable Britain to retain Kenya as a colony. Once the process was underway, this objective would change.

The first truly significant step in that direction came in 1954 with the Lyttleton Constitution. This created a new structure for central government based on the principle of multiracial representation and a ministerial system that included both African and Asian ministers. Britain's strategy was to integrate the Kenyan 'middle classes' into the colonial order and thus hold shared interests under British control. The actual effect was to show Kenyan nationalists that the status quo was changing and progress towards independence could be realistically made. Each constitutional restructuring that the colonial authorities presented was rejected, as was the Lyttleton Constitution.

Political pressure for decolonisation

Even as late as 1959, the Colonial Secretary, Lennox-Boyd, stated that Kenya would achieve independence no earlier than 1975. By February 1960, Macmillan announced what appeared to be a complete U-turn in British imperial policy in Africa. The question is to what extent did non-Mau Mau nationalist-based political pressure influence Britain's actions in Kenya from 1960? In June 1955, political parties were allowed to function at district level but national consciousness was underdeveloped and most Kenyans lacked any experience in party organisation. This allowed a nationalist political elite to develop.

Elections held in 1957 under the Lyttleton Constitution projected a new generation of African nationalist politicians to the forefront of Kenyan nationalism. Amongst them were Tom Mboya, Oginga Odinga and Daniel arap Moi. Mboya was an articulate trade unionist who had written *The Kenya Question – An African Answer* (1956). His election slogan was, 'To hell with European domination'. This group, and others, immediately formed the African Elected Members Organisation (AEMO) and rejected the constitution.

The nationalists undoubtedly held the initiative after **the Hola Camp massacre** in March 1959. The new Colonial Secretary, Ian Macleod, admitted that 'Hola helped to convince me that swift change was needed in Kenya'. The imperial government had no coordinated policies in place to respond to nationalist pressure. The problem for the nationalists was that they were not united. In 1959, the Kenya National Party (KNP) was formed, quickly followed by the Kenya Independence Movement (KIM). Despite this, Britain accepted the principle of African majority rule in Kenya at the first Lancaster House Conference in January 1960. After this first conference, the two main nationalist parties were formed. These were the Kenyan African National Union (KANU) and the Kenyan African

KEY EVENT

The Hola Camp Massacre, 1959
Hola was a detention camp used to hold Mau Mau terrorist suspects. On March 3, 1959 a group of detainees were ordered to carry out digging work. They refused on the grounds that they were political prisoners. The British guards reacted with extreme violence against the prisoners and this resulted in 11 deaths. The incident led to a huge amount of political opposition to the government in Britain.

Democratic Union (KADU). KANU was the more radical of the two and in August 1961 Kenyatta became its first official leader upon his release from detention. From this point, the road to independence was mapped out. Political nationalism exploited the fractures that the Mau Mau had created in colonial rule in Kenya. Without the Mau Mau, independence may well have taken much longer to achieve, but in itself it was necessary but not sufficient to ensure independence. That came through the political determination of men such as Odinga and Mboya. On 12 December 1963, the Union Jack was brought down as Kenya's national black, red, green and white flag was hoisted.

Uganda

Tribal differences, which were expressed through social class conflict and ethnic cultural divisions, impeded any sense of national unity in Uganda. Initially, the voice of Ugandan nationalism was largely stifled by these divisions. However, the rationale underlying the nationalist response to colonial rule in Uganda was not dissimilar from that applied in other African states. After the Second World War, the price of Ugandan cotton fell and the country experienced rising inflation in consumer goods. National awareness developed rapidly in the certainty that Britain was undermining Ugandan Africans' economic opportunities. Basically, the relationship with Britain was perceived as being economically damaging rather than economically advantageous to Africans.

Mutesa

The most powerful tribal group in Uganda were the Buganda, led after the war by their young king, Mutesa. The focus of Buganda-inspired nationalism was upon preventing themselves from being merged into a large unitary Ugandan state. The Buganda wanted a federal Uganda in order to protect their own interests. Mutesa was not campaigning for a unitary and independent Ugandan state but British actions served to heighten his nationalist credentials. Mutesa was a tribal aristocrat who represented only one ethnic section within Uganda. He was seen by many Ugandans as an indirect agent of colonial rule. His identity with the rest of African Ugandan society was tenuous and as such his ability to act as a national leader was meagre. By placing Mutesa under arrest and forcing him into exile in Britain in 1953, the colonial authorities transformed Mutesa into a Ugandan nationalist leader.

Other groups

The Roman Catholic Church formed the focal point around which many nationalist groups gravitated. The Church had traditionally opposed colonialism and its network of missions offered an excellent base from which to spread the nationalist message across the whole country. The northern region of Uganda also had its nationalist politicians who formed a 'people's congress', which aimed to establish a united Ugandan nation. It was through this diverse coalition of nationalist groups that Milton Obote became the first Prime Minister of an independent Uganda in 1962. Once again, a groundswell of popular nationalism had succeeded in winning independence. In spite of Mutesa's nationalist political discourse, Uganda was non-elitist and the nationalist message was able to reach a very large proportion of 'ordinary' Ugandans. In Uganda, the task of achieving independence was made easier through the absence of a large white settler population whose interests would have had to be considered by the colonial authorities.

Tanganyika

This was a large state with a relatively small population. The key to the development of nationalism lay in the fact that, unlike in many other African tribal states, there was a common language spoken. This was Swahili and it formed the basis of the spread of national consciousness. Nationalist leaders could readily access the ordinary people regardless of their tribal differences. A common language meant that communications were more open and geographically scattered. The vast majority of Tanganyikans could participate in the nationalist debate and were therefore more inclined to adopt an activist stance. Tanganyika's nationalist leader, Julius Nyerere, was typical of the educated African nationalists who had absorbed democratic socialist thinking in Britain during the 1930s and transmitted this to his own country. This style of political communication appealed to the Tanganyikan masses.

The Central African Federation

In 1953, Britain created a new federal organisation in Africa consisting of Northern and Southern Rhodesia and Nyasaland. In part, this was done to prevent Southern Rhodesia being drawn into the orbit of South Africa where Afrikaner nationalists had taken power in 1948. White nationalism was a powerful force in South Africa. There were 300,000 whites in Northern and Southern Rhodesia and more arrived after 1945. This white nationalism was encouraged by the growth of black nationalism elsewhere in Africa. Nyasaland was made up almost entirely of native black Africans. Macmillan later commented:

> Had any of us realised the most revolutionary way in which the situation would develop, and the rapid growth of African nationalism throughout the whole African continent, I think I should have opposed the putting together of three countries so opposite in their character and so different in their history.

Nyasaland

In 1959, revolt erupted in Nyasaland, led by Hastings Banda. The primary motivating factor that drove Banda was the conviction that without independence Nyasaland's people would be forever subordinate to the rule of white Rhodesians within the federation. Banda's leadership was the catalyst that produced independence. He said, 'Moderates have never achieved anything. It took extremists like Oliver Cromwell and Mrs Pankhurst to get things done.' Banda's party created a state within a state in Nyasaland as the nationalists simply boycotted the capital and refused to cooperate with government officials. Over the next four years, power was transferred to the nationalists and in 1964 the independent state of Malawi was created. Nationalism had been very effective but the primary reason for its success lay in the recognition by Britain that Nyasaland had no significance in terms of British interests in South Africa. Economically, it was of little value compared to the copper mines of Northern Rhodesia and the tobacco and maize plantations of the South.

Northern Rhodesia

In Northern Rhodesia, the nationalist leader Kenneth Kaunda was as determined in his extremism as Banda. Kaunda threatened to make the Mau Mau campaigns look like a 'child's picnic'. Again, although nationalism did have a significant impact on Britain's decision to decolonise in Northern Rhodesia, there were powerful economic factors that supported nationalism. Britain feared the loss of cheap Rhodesian copper but was convinced that the favourable terms of trade would be unaffected by independence. The new state of Zambia would remain economically dependent upon the sale of copper to Britain. In effect, little of real significance changed for Britain. Black majority rule had no major impact on what really mattered to Britain, therefore Britain could afford to comply with African nationalism and avoid unnecessary conflict. The economic context and the inevitable collapse of the federation made it almost impossible for nationalism not to succeed in Northern Rhodesia.

Southern Rhodesia

White nationalism was the power source in Southern Rhodesia. Faced with Britain's determination not to offend the Afro–Asian Commonwealth by supporting what was perceived as white supremacy in Southern Rhodesia, the Prime Minister, Ian Smith, made a Unilateral Declaration in Independence (UDI) in November 1965.

Rhodesian Africans made it clear that they would not accept independence without black majority rule. Black nationalism fought in exile. Zapu, led by Joshua Nkomo, was based in Zambia, while its rival, Zanu, led by Robert Mugabe, operated from Mozambique. Mugabe was determined not to simply inherit an intact colonial structure. He wanted to establish a new egalitarian society. South Africa feared that an armed struggle between these two groups might spill over into its apartheid system and so became increasingly concerned that a peaceful resolution be reached sooner rather than later. Ian Smith was also convinced that the war had to be resolved. In 1980, Mugabe was appointed the Prime Minister of an independent Zimbabwe.

Aggressive nationalism had been successful. Mozambique had played a key role but the negative perceptions of white supremacy, which was increasingly being rejected internationally, was also a factor. The apartheid system in South Africa was no longer acceptable and due to lack of international support Rhodesia's determination to prevent majority rule could not succeed.

NATIONALISM IN THE FAR EAST

Malaya

By January 1942, the Japanese army was advancing almost unopposed down the Malayan Peninsular. On 15 February 1942, about 70,000 imperial troops surrendered the 'Gibraltar of the East', Singapore, to the Japanese after a mere fifteen days of resistance. The territorial and military losses, serious though they were, paled into insignificance compared to the impact the defeat was to have upon the perception of British imperial rule, not just in Malaya but also throughout the British Empire. The British had cultivated an ethos of superiority that was instantly shattered by the Japanese occupation. There is no doubt that Britain's defeat at the hands of an Asiatic state, Japan, significantly undermined Britain's image as an invincible western imperial power. The defeat also heightened the realisation that Britain no longer had the military capacity to maintain such far flung imperial outposts. Malaya proved that geographically Britain's empire was too scattered to defend effectively. To add to this, the Japanese occupiers of Malaya and Burma encouraged the development of nationalist groups by establishing puppet regimes.

The immediate post-war situation in Malaya was similar to that in Africa. An economic crisis based on inflation, food shortages and unemployment dogged British attempts to restore imperial credibility in Malaya. The Malayan population consisted not only of indigenous peoples but a significant proportion of ethnic Chinese and Indians who had emigrated to Malaya for economic reasons during the nineteenth century. In 1948, the Malayan Communist Party organised strikes amongst the groups who worked on the rubber plantations and in the tin mines. N. White offers a useful comment on this in his work *Decolonisation: The British Experience Since 1945* (1999) when he notes, 'To present the communist revolt as a nationalist uprising is problematic since the MCP was largely a Chinese chauvinist organisation and did not appeal to the Malays.'

What stimulated nationalist fervour in Malaya more than anything was the application of a multi-racialist policy adopted by Britain. A similar approach had been tried in East Africa during the 1950s. Britain proposed a Malaya Union that threatened to jeopardise Malay political supremacy. Malay nationalism was perhaps more complex than any other within the British Empire. In his work *The Invention of Politics in Colonial Malaya* (1994), A. Milner suggests that 'even in the last years of the British presence, the character and value of (Malay) nationalism continued to be a matter of debate'. Malay nationalism became a complex compromise between the Malay race, Malay Chinese, Malay Indians and the Sultanate. Although a contributory factor, nationalism in Malaya played a far less significant role in the achievement of independence than did nationalism in other parts of the British Empire, particularly in India and Africa. Malay nationalism was too diverse and too sectional to have a major impact. Although there was terrorism, its impact was significantly less influential in contributing towards independence than the Mau Mau was in Kenya, for example.

CONCLUSIONS

All European imperial powers were confronted with nationalist movements and the British experience was no exception to this. Nationalism was a means of political expression that was available to largely disenfranchised indigenous peoples. It was often the product of rising populations faced with diminishing resources, agricultural depression and economic deprivation. Many colonial peoples would have remained content with their colonial lot if conditions had improved for them. Nationalism may well have remained a fringe concept that inspired only a small number of articulate middle class activists.

The post-war order that Britain entered revealed the growing international and economic irrelevancy of maintaining a massive global empire. A new, more rational and pragmatic relationship had to be established and it was this fracture in imperial normality that nationalism was able to exploit to great effect. The post-war context offered an ideal environment for nationalism in all its forms to be used positively.

At times, nationalism was divisive. It expressed itself through terror and, although this did have an impact, it often delayed the moves towards independence. However, the reality for most forms of nationalism was that there had to be a degree of determination that could only be effectively expressed through violence.

A2 ASSESSMENT

SOURCE BASED QUESTIONS IN THE STYLE OF AQA

Read the following sources and then answer the questions that follow.

Source A

From a public opinion poll interview conducted by Mass Observation, September 1938:

Middle-aged man: Britain should not support Czechoslovakia, even if Germany acts as it did towards Austria. Chamberlain has tried to mediate and that was what everybody wanted.

Source B

The 'gap' between the government and public opinion was most clearly perceived following the German coup against Prague in March 1939. To the former, Hitler's fresh act of aggression was regrettable but nothing more. The first reactions of Chamberlain, Halifax and Simon were therefore complacent. The explosion of discontent that followed, in the Conservative Party and in traditional pro-government papers like *The Observer*, forced a sudden change of tone; by 17 March, Chamberlain was publicly warning that 'any attempt to dominate the world by force was one which the democracies must resist'.

Adapted from *The Realities Behind Diplomacy*, Paul Kennedy (1981)

Questions

Before answering these questions, you should read Section 1. All the questions require you to use **both** your own knowledge and the sources.

In responding effectively to source based questions, it is very important that you avoid simply paraphrasing the content of the source. Identify the key words in the question and plan your answer. Many candidates make the mistaken assumption that a plan is only needed for essay type answers. If for no other reason, a plan is useful in enabling you to see at a glance whether or not you have considered the source and your own knowledge and if you have done more than recycle the information in the source.

(a) Use **Source A** and your own knowledge.

How useful is this source for an historian studying British public opinion during the Munich crisis in September 1938? (10 marks)

How to answer this question

This question is asking you to assess the utility of the source in terms of understanding accurately the condition of British public opinion. Implicit in this type of question is the limitations of the source's usefulness and the problems this could create for an historian conducting a study of public opinion.

- You may summarise the content of the source and suggest public opinion backed appeasement as far as Czechoslovakia was concerned. Clearly this would not be addressing the key issue of source utility, nor would it be based on any 'own knowledge'. A more developed and focused response is needed for higher marks.

- The source offers only one person's viewpoint. This immediately weakens its usefulness as an indicator of national opinion. There are a series of other limitations that could be highlighted in order to illustrate the problems an historian might face when using this source. Who is the respondent? What is his social background? What political party did he support? What newspaper did he read? Other issues could include some reference to the problems of extrapolation. Can historians write accurate interpretations based on such a narrow and underdeveloped response to one specific question? Reference to your own knowledge might be used to suggest that many people actually opposed the view expressed in the source. You could include some detailed information to support this.

(b) Use **Sources A and B** and your own knowledge.

To what extent do you agree with the view that the British government responded positively to public opinion when determining the course of British foreign policy between 1937 and 1939? (20 marks)

How to answer this question

You must refer to **both** the sources. Source A suggests popular support, but it is not clear whether the government has reacted to or created the opinion. Source B does suggest a positive shift in policy in response to opinion but it also suggests that there was little real understanding of popular opinion before March 1939, or at least there was little inclination to want to understand it.

- A good approach would be to use your own knowledge to consider the problems of determining whether the government manipulated opinion or reacted to it. There is also the issue of whether the government viewed appeasement as a viable long-term policy. Rearmament was underway. Was the Czech situation in March 1939 really a policy turning point? Did the government react so conclusively to opinion as Source B suggests, or had it already considered the possibility of a further Czech crisis?

- You are being asked to assess the extent to which a view is correct. You must conclude with a judgement that measures this and is sustained by evidence in the body of your answer.

SOURCE BASED QUESTIONS IN THE STYLE OF EDEXCEL

Source 1
Adapted from a speech delivered by Lord Rosebery in 1893.

It is said that our empire is already large enough and does not need extension. That would be true enough if the world was elastic, but it is not. At present, we are 'pegging out' our claims for the future. We have to remember that it is part of our heritage to take care that the world is moulded by us and that it shall receive an English-speaking complexion and not that of other nations. We have to look forward to the future of our race. We should fail in our duty if we decline to take our share of the partition of the world.

Source 2
From a Cabinet minute taken on 27 July 1956.

The fundamental question before the Cabinet was whether they were prepared to pursue their objective by the use of force. The Cabinet agreed that our essential interests in this area must be safeguarded by military action and that the necessary preparations to this end must be made. Failure to hold the Suez Canal would inevitably lead to the loss, one by one, of all our assets in the Middle East.

Source 3
Adapted from a speech delivered by Harold Macmillan in February 1960.

Since the end of the war, the processes that gave birth to the nation states of Europe have been repeated all over the world. We have seen the awakening of national consciousness in peoples who have for centuries lived in dependence upon some other power. Today this is happening in Africa. The wind of change is blowing through this continent and, whether we like it or not, this growth of national consciousness is a political fact. We must all accept it as a fact, and our national policies must take account of it.

Questions
Before answering these questions, it would be useful to read Sections 2–4. A key approach to these questions is to remember that they focus on change over time and the notion of events representing major turning points that contribute to that change. Not only is change central to these questions but also the ideas of limited change or continuity.

> **(a)** Use your own knowledge.
>
> How far do you agree that the Suez Crisis (1956) marked a turning point in British imperial policy? (20 marks)

How to answer this question
You need to read the relevant part of Section 3. The focus is on your own knowledge and your ability to analyse the significance of the event in terms of change and continuity. Again, it would be useful to use the mark allocation as a guide to detail and length.

- In order to establish the extent of the 'turning point', you need to consider the positions before and after the event. Avoid writing a long narrative of the details of the Suez Crisis itself. Remain focused on the key words in the question.
- There is a considerable amount of historiographic material on this topic and this could be usefully exploited in the answer. You need to assess the relationship Britain had with the USA and the impact of this in the post-Suez world. Did Suez really fundamentally redirect British policy, or did it simply contribute to a policy direction that was already in place? It is worth noting that there is no clear-cut and definitive answer to this question. Essentially, the examiners are looking for your ability to construct a balanced and coherent argument that leads to a viable judgement. They are not looking for narrative detail and unsupported responses that are predominantly based on assertions.

(b) Study **Sources 1, 2** and **3** and use your own knowledge.

How far do you agree with the view that it was perceptions of Britain's national interests that provide the key to explaining both the expansion and the contraction of Britain's empire in Africa?

How to answer this question

This is about change over time and it requires you to use not only the sources but also your own knowledge. You should remain focused on the key words. In this case, these draw you to Africa and not the rest of the empire. They also ask you to examine the changing nature of British policy and the motives underlying that change. No specific factor, such as economic issues, is identified; therefore you must examine a range of issues.

- The 40 marks available for this question are divided into two sections: 16 marks for an analysis of the sources and 24 marks for the application of your own knowledge.
- You can use the sources to establish what motivated British policy from the late nineteenth century up to the high watermark of decolonisation in the 1960s. You need to explain these motives primarily in the context of economic and strategic factors. A useful practical approach is to take each source in turn. An analysis must not degenerate into a simple description. The sources will provide evidence and it is this that must be explained in terms of the question.
- A survey of changing priorities could be developed through your own knowledge. It could also draw on elements of continuity. The key issue could be that Britain always viewed its empire in terms of its own national interest and it policies simply moulded around changing perceptions of what was in Britain's national interests at any given point in time during this period.
- In this question, as in the previous one, it is essential to arrive at a coherent and reasoned judgement.

BIBLIOGRAPHY

The books in this bibliography have been listed in terms of their relevancy to each of the two sections in this book. Many of the references used in the AS section could be used effectively for the A2 section and vice versa. This is a selective bibliography and is in no sense exhaustive.

AS SECTION

H. Browne, *Joseph Chamberlain, Radical and Imperialist* (Longman, 1974)

M. Chamberlain, *Pax Britannica* (Modern History Review, September 1996)

M. Chamberlain, *The Scramble for Africa* (Longman, 1974)

G. Clayton, *Britain and the Eastern Question* (University of London Press, 1971)

A. Farmer, *British Foreign and Imperial Affairs, 1939–1964* (Hodder and Stoughton, 1994)

D.K. Fieldhouse, *Economics and Empire, 1830–1914* (Macmillan, 1984)

S. Greenwood, *Britain and the Cold War 1945 to 1991* (Macmillan, 2000)

D. Judd and P. Slinn, *The Evolution of the Modern Commonwealth* (Macmillan, 1982)

J.M. Mackenzie, *Propaganda and the Empire, 1880 – 1960* (Manchester University Press, 1984)

R. Pearce, *Britain and the European Powers, 1865–1914* (Hodder and Stoughton, 1996)

A. Porter (ed.), *The Oxford History of the British Empire: The 19th Century* (OUP, 1999)

G. Thorn, *End of Empires: European Decolonisation 1919-80* (Hodder and Stoughton, 2000)

D.W. Urwin, *Western Europe since 1945* (Longman, 1991)

J.W. Young, *Britain and European Unity, 1945-1992* (Macmillan, 1993)

A2 SECTION

G. Almond, *The American People and Foreign Policy* (New York, 1977)

D. Birmingham, *Decolonisation in Africa* (UCL Press, 1995)

P.J. Cain and A.J. Hopkins, *British Imperialism: Innovation and Expansion, 1688–1914* (Longman, 1993)

P.J. Cain and A.J. Hopkins, *British Imperialism: Crisis and Destruction, 1914–1990* (Longman, 1993)

W. Churchill, *The Gathering Storm* (Cassell, 1948)

J. Darwin, *Britain and Decolonisation: The Retreat from Empire in the Post-War World* (Macmillan, 1988)

J. Darwin, *The End of the British Empire: The Historical Debate* (Blackwell, 1991)

P. Finney (ed.), *The Origins of the Second World War* (Arnold, 1997)

J. Hargreaves, *Decolonisation in Africa* (Longman 1988)

E. Hobsbawn *The Age of Empire 1875–1914* (Abacus, 1994)

J.A. Hobson, *Imperialism: A Study* (London, 1902)

R.F. Holland, *The Pursuit of Greatness: Britain and the World Role, 1900–1970* (Fontana, 1991)

K.J. Holsti, *International Politics: A Framework for Analysis* (Prentice Hall, 1994)

P. Kennedy, *The Rise and Fall of the Great Powers* (Unwin Hyman, 1988)

P. Kennedy, *The Realities Behind Diplomacy* (Fontana, 1989)

B. Lapping, *Did Suez Hasten the End of Empire?* (Contemporary Record Vol. 1 No. 2, 1987)

R. Long, *The Man on the Spot* (Greenwood Press, 1995)

P. Marshall, *Imperialism* (History Sixth, No. 6, March 1990)

F. McDonough, *The British Empire 1815–1914* (Hodder and Stoughton, 1994)

F. McDonough, *Neville Chamberlain, Appeasement and the British Road to War* (Manchester University Press, 1998)

B.A. Ogot and W.R. Ochieng (ed.), *Decolonisation and Independence in Kenya, 1940–93* (James Currey, 1995)

R.A.C. Parker, *Chamberlain and Appeasement* (Macmillan, 1993)

H. Pelling, *Popular Politics in the Late Victorian Age* (Macmillan, 1967)

A.N. Porter, *The Origins of the South African War: Joseph Chamberlain and the Diplomacy of Imperialism, 1895–1899* (Manchester, 1980)

R. Price, *An Imperial War and the Working Class* (London, 1972)

E. Ranson, *British Defence Policy and Appeasement Between the Wars, 1919–1939* (Historical Association, 1993)

D. Reynolds, *Britannia Overruled: British Policy and World Power in the Twentieth Century* (Longman, 1991)

R. Robinson and J. Gallagher, *Africans and Victorians: The Official Mind of Imperialism* (London, 1961)

R. Robinson and J. Gallagher, *The Imperialism of Free Trade* (Economic History Review, Vol. 6.1, 1953)

R. Shannon, *Crisis of Imperialism* (London, 1977)

N. Smart, *The National Government, 1931–40* (Palgrave Macmillan, 1999)

A.J.P. Taylor, *The Origins of the Second World War* (Penguin, 1961)

A.J.P. Taylor, *The Struggle for Mastery in Europe* (OUP, 1954)

N. White, *Decolonisation: The British Experience since 1945* (Longman, 1999)

R.W. Winks (ed.), *The Oxford History of the British Empire: Historiography* (OUP, 1999)

Page numbers in italics refer to maps.

HEINEMANN ADVANCED HISTORY